THE PAST IN PERSPECTIVE

CAPITALISM, COMMUNITY AND CONFLICT

THE SOUTH WALES COALFIELD, 1898–1947

Chris Williams

CARDIFF
UNIVERSITY OF WALES PRESS
1998

British Library Cataloguing-In-Publication Data.
A catalogue record for this book is available from the British
Library.

ISBN (paperback) 0-7083-1473-2
      (cased) 0-7083-1493-7

Typeset at the University of Wales Press
Printed in Great Britain by Dinefwr Press, Llandybïe

THE PAST IN PERSPECTIVE

Series Editors: C. C. Eldridge and Ralph A. Griffiths

CAPITALISM, COMMUNITY AND CONFLICT

THE PAST IN PERSPECTIVE

Series Editors: C. C. Eldridge and Ralph A. Griffiths

C. C. Eldridge is Reader in History at the University of Wales, Lampeter.

Ralph A. Griffiths is Professor of Medieval History at the University of Wales, Swansea.

In memory of my grandparents, all inhabitants of the south Wales coalfield:

Annie Rogers (née Standley), 1910–1976
Joseph Rogers, 1901–1947
Sarah Catherine Williams (née Hale), 1909–1991
Harry Williams, 1906–1967

Contents

Editors' Foreword

Each volume in this series, *The Past in Perspective*, deals with a major theme of British, European or World history. The aim of the series is to engage the interest of all for whom knowledge of the riches of the world's historical experience is a delight, and in particular to meet the needs of students of history in universities and colleges — and at comparatively modest cost.

Each theme is tackled at sufficient length and in sufficient depth to allow each writer both to advance our understanding of the subject in the light of the most recent research, and to place his or her approach in due perspective. Accordingly, each volume contains a historiographical chapter which assesses how interpretations of its theme have developed, and have been criticized, endorsed, modified or discarded. Each volume, too, includes a section of substantial excerpts from key original sources: this reflects the importance of allowing the reader to come to his or her own conclusions about differing interpretations, and also the greater accessibility nowadays of original sources in print. Furthermore, in each volume there is a detailed bibliography which not only underpins the writer's own account and analysis, but also enables the reader to pursue the theme, or particular aspects of it, to even greater depth; the explosion of historical writing in the twentieth century makes such guidance invaluable. By these perspectives, taken together, each volume is an up-to-date, authoritative and substantial exploration of themes, ancient, medieval or modern, of British, European, American or World significance, after more than a century of the study and teaching of history.

C. C. Eldridge and Ralph A. Griffiths

Explanatory note
Reference to the Illustrative Documents which follow the main text are indicated by a bold roman numeral preceded by the word 'DOCUMENT', all within square brackets [**DOCUMENT XII**].

Acknowledgements

In writing this volume I have amassed debts which are only barely
repaid with a word of thanks. The series editors Ralph Griffiths and
Colin Eldridge have given encouragement and clear direction; at the
University of Wales Press Ceinwen Jones, Susan Jenkins, Janet
Davies, and Dean Mitchell have prompted, organized and refined my
labours; Ian Dennis and Howard Mason of the School of History
and Archaeology have converted my sketches into legible maps; and
Elisabeth Bennett of the South Wales Coalfield Archive and Siân
Williams of the South Wales Miners' Library have given generously
of their time and expertise in helping me to locate relevant material.

Amongst my many comrades, colleagues and friends I would like
to express my gratitude to Bill Jones, Andy Croll and Angela Gaffney
in particular. Josephine Williams, Peter Williams, Harri Williams and
Sara Spalding have again tolerated my absorption in my work: their
constant support has been indispensable.

Of my grandparents, to whom this work is dedicated, only one
lived to see me become a historian of the society they all inhabited. I
would like to believe that, in these pages, they might have recognized
at least an element of their own experiences.

The author and publishers wish to thank the following for kind
permission to reproduce extracts in this volume:

Document I: Viv Davies for the extract from 'Miners' Town' by
B. L. Coombes.

Document VIII: South Wales Coalfield Collection, University of
Wales Swansea Library & Information Services, for the interview
with Will Paynter.

Document XII: Christopher Davies Publishers Ltd, Swansea, for
the extract from *Ups and Downs* by Walter Haydn Davies (1975).

Document XVIII: Rosemary Scadden for the extract from her
M.Sc.Econ thesis.

Document XXI: Copyright the Trustees of the Mass-Observation
Archive at the University of Sussex, reproduced with permission of
Curtis Brown Ltd, London.

Every effort has been made to trace the copyright holders of
substantial extracts in this volume. In the case of any queries, please
contact the publishers.

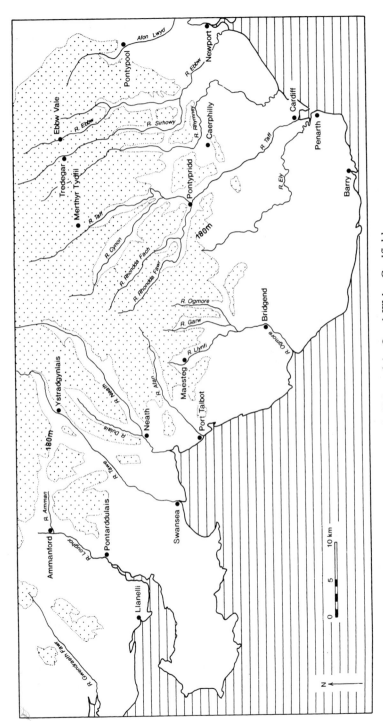

Map 1: Relief Map of the South Wales Coalfield

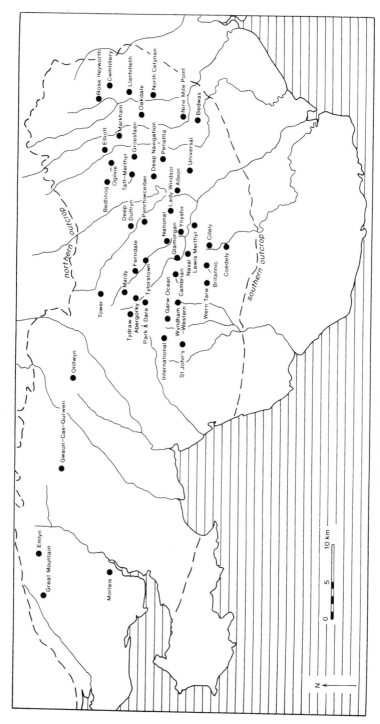

Map 2: Major Collieries mentioned in the Text

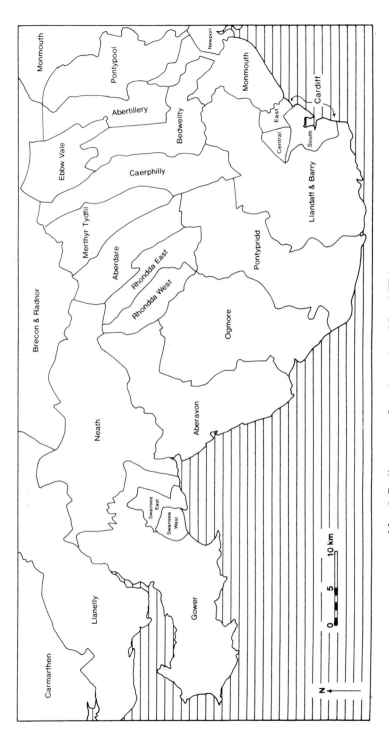

Map 3: Parliamentary Constituencies of South Wales, 1918–1945

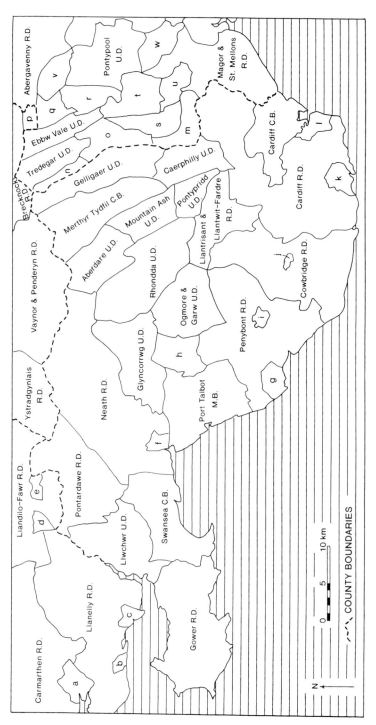

Map 4: Local Government Areas of South Wales, 1937

Carmarthen R.D.

Llanelly R.D.

Llandilo-Fawr R.D.

Pontardawe R.D.

Llwchwr U.D.

Swansea C.B.

Gower R.D.

Ystradgynlais R.D.

Neath R.D.

Glyncorrwg U.D.

Port Talbot M.B.

Vaynor & Penderyn R.D.

Aberdare U.D.

Rhondda U.D.

Ogmore & Garw U.D.

Penybont R.D.

Cowbridge R.D.

Merthyr Tydfil C.B.

Mountain Ash U.D.

Pontypridd U.D.

Llantrisant & Llantwit-Fardre R.D.

Brecknock R.D.

Tredegar U.D.

Gelligaer U.D.

Caerphilly U.D.

Ebbw Vale U.D.

Abergavenny R.D.

Pontypool U.D.

Magor & St. Mellons R.D.

Cardiff C.B.

Cardiff R.D.

N

0   5   10 km

- - - COUNTY BOUNDARIES

a
b
c
d
e
f
g
h
i
j
k
l
m
n
o
p
q
r
s
t
u
v
w

Key to Map 4

a Kidwelly Municipal Borough
b Burry Port Urban District
c Llanelly MB
d Ammanford UD
e Cwmamman UD
f Neath MB
g Porthcawl UD

h Maesteg UD
i Bridgend UD
j Cowbridge MB
k Barry UD
l Penarth UD
m Bedwas and Machen UD
n Rhymney UD
o Bedwellty UD

p Brynmawr UD
q Nantyglo and Blaina UD
r Abertillery UD
s Mynyddislwyn UD
t Abercarn UD
u Risca UD
v Blaenavon UD
w Cwmbran UD

Abbreviations

AAM	Amalgamated Association of Mineworkers
BUF	British Union of Fascists
CLP	Constituency Labour Party
ILP	Independent Labour Party
MFGB	Mineworkers' Federation of Great Britain
MSWCOA	Monmouthshire and South Wales Coal Owners' Association
NCB	National Coal Board
NUM	National Union of Mineworkers
(SW)MIU	(South Wales) Miners' Industrial Union
SWMF	South Wales Miners' Federation (or the 'Fed')
TUC	Trades Union Congress

1.   Historical Perspectives

An assessment of the history of the south Wales coalfield must acknowledge that the coalfield was primarily an economic phenomenon. And
the story of the coalfield's past has mirrored the rise and decline of the
coal industry. After pioneering work on the early nineteenth century in
A. H. John's *The Industrial Development of South Wales, 1750–1850*
(1950), the critical decades of the 1840s to the 1870s, which saw the
deep-mine industry established, were given authoritative treatment by
J. H. Morris and L. J. Williams in *The South Wales Coal Industry,
1841–1875* (1958). John Williams has since produced equally important assessments of more recent developments, drawing economic,
industrial relations and trade-union histories together in exemplary
fashion (see his *Was Wales Industrialised?* (1995)), and his work has
been complemented by that of Rhodri Walters (particularly in *The
Economic and Business History of the South Wales Steam Coal Industry,
1840–1914* (1977)). Other historians, including Martin Daunton and
Trevor Boyns, have deepened our understanding of the nature of the
work process underground, of its attendant dangers, of the complex
interaction of industry and war economies, and of the reactions of the
coal industry to stagnation and decline in the decades between the
world wars. The most successful approach to estimating the place of
the coal industry in the wider economy of south Wales can be found in
Industrial Glamorgan, the fifth volume of the *Glamorgan County History*
(edited by Arthur H. John and Glanmor Williams (1980)), which
managed to integrate coal with iron, transport, capital, labour supply
and agriculture; unfortunately, similar treatments for Monmouthshire
and Carmarthenshire have yet to be undertaken. At the level of an
individual industrial community, E. D. Lewis's magnificent *The
Rhondda Valleys* (1958) explored its archetypal subject in an equally
integrated manner, and it still stands peerless forty years on.
　　Despite the high quality of much of this work, the study of the
economic history of the south Wales coalfield is beginning to appear

in danger of exhaustion. The 'advanced technology' of the 'new economic history' has had little impact on Welsh scholarship, although, given its complexity, this may be a blessing in disguise. Of greater concern is the apparent absence of a new generation of scholars who might return to half-worked seams of research or open new ones. An even-handed approach to the entrepreneurial and business history of the coalfield, from the mid-nineteenth century through to nationalization and beyond, remains a major gap, as does a history of the steel industry in south Wales. Work on the geographical and spatial context of economic development needs to build on the solid foundations laid down by Philip Jones, *Colliery Settlement in the South Wales Coalfield, 1850–1926* (1969). The findings and arguments of economic historians who study the coal industry in Britain as a whole, and its comparative international dimension, demand a response from those who study a society that once exported its 'black diamonds' on a global scale. Deian Hopkin observed in 1987 that in modern Welsh history '[t]here are far too many empty shelves, where studies of demography, migration, standards of living, patterns of consumption, health, welfare and education should sit'.[1] More than a decade later little has changed, and although it is difficult to be precise about the relationships between economic change and social and political developments, no historian of the south Wales coalfield and its society should neglect the economic domain. The publication of the *Digest of Welsh Historical Statistics* (1985) allows no excuses to those who fail to pay attention to the trends and movements which it outlines. Whatever the lacunae or opaqueness of the statistical series, whatever the difficulty of interpreting human actions from a run of aggregates or averages, an understanding of economic change must be an integral element of this history.

Already at the centre of much of the written history of the coalfield stand the south Wales miners and their trade union, the South Wales Miners' Federation (SWMF). Founded in 1898 following a six-month lockout, and entering a newly nationalized industry on 1 January 1947, the turbulent experiences of this large body of organized workers determine the chronological parameters of this book. The south Wales miners have been extremely well served by a series of deeply committed, often highly politicized historians. Ness Edwards, a miners' agent, and later a SWMF-sponsored Labour MP, writing in the 1920s and 1930s, saw his histories (*The History of the South Wales Miners* (1926); *The History of the South Wales Miners'*

Federation (1938)) as didactic: 'the modern Welsh miner will better assess the value of his trade union by knowing what tremendous tasks it has performed in the past'. Operating from within the other major political tradition in the coalfield of the twentieth century, the Communist Party, Robin Page Arnot, himself a veteran and leading Communist, penned the first two 'official' histories of the south Wales miners (*South Wales Miners, I: 1898–1914* (1967); *South Wales Miners, II: 1914–1926* (1975)). Both authors wrote with inside knowledge of the union, and had great sympathy with its objectives. Subsequent historians owe their books a major debt for they assembled a substantial body of scholarship, and remain a regular point of reference for any institutional history of the SWMF. Yet whatever their contribution to the historical record, the conceptualization, assumptions and tenor of their works no longer appear satisfactory. Page Arnot in particular wrote from a standpoint which viewed the miners' history as one of lengthy and bitter struggle leading to eventual triumph, as private ownership was replaced by the National Coal Board, and regional miners' unions were succeeded by a single National Union of Mineworkers (NUM). Today that process of historical evolution appears contingent rather than natural, and the triumphal tone is overlaid with the irony of privatization, the shredding of the NUM and the virtual extinction of the deep-mine industry in south Wales. Both Edwards and Page Arnot took for granted the identification of ordinary miners with their union and its policies, and showed scant concern for any life outside union structures: there was little sense of miners having families or leisure time, of mixing with other workers, or of coal owners and colliery managers as anything more than the unacceptable face of capitalism. These one-dimensional histories still stand as important waymarks, but it is unlikely that many historians will wish to follow closely in their steps.

The third volume of the 'official' history of the south Wales miners, *The Fed: A History of the South Wales Miners in the Twentieth Century* (1980), by Hywel Francis and David Smith, belongs to a different era and a different class of historical scholarship. *The Fed* has to be understood as part of an important attempt to reclaim and preserve selected aspects, artefacts and memories of the coalfield's past. This book took shape in the form of a funded project to collect oral testimonies, minute books and other documentary evidence, as well as to rescue the contents of many miners' institute libraries from destruction. Outcomes of the project included the establishment of the South Wales Miners' Library and the South Wales Coalfield Archive at Swansea. Running parallel, and involving much overlap in personnel, was the foundation of Llafur: the Welsh Labour History Society, and the issue of its annual journal from 1972 onwards. A critical mass of research, debate and interest was generated, and has been sustained to the present day. *The Fed* merits praise for its striking methodology, its textured scholarship and its captivating style. Although it remained a trade-union history, the union's relationship to – indeed its centrality within – the wider society was a prominent theme. The institutional shackles of Edwards and Page Arnot were broken, and internal debates, factional conflicts and strategic tensions explored. Oral evidence taken often from participants in key struggles was interwoven with the more muted testimonies of the minute books, newspapers and government reports. Finally, the intimate knowledge which the authors had of the society under discussion, *their* society, suffused *The Fed* with an eloquent passion and gave it an authenticity that few historians can aspire to match.

Inevitably, judgements arrived at in 1980 have been reassessed and revised, and new researches have supplemented, enhanced, corrected or modified the work of Francis and Smith. The fact that *The Fed* was conceptualized and written in the aftermath of the successful miners' strikes of 1972 and 1974, and before the catastrophic defeat of 1984–5, may account for the occasional argument that may now seem unjustifiably boisterous or over-optimistic. The focus on the 'union in its society' is revelatory, but it carries with it the danger that those elements of the society not directly linked to the SWMF (including many women) may have to struggle to have their voices heard. Within the authors' own terms of reference, it is their characterization of coalfield society as an 'alternative culture', and as exhibiting 'proletarian internationalism', that remains at once stimulating and controversial.

The coalfield's 'alternative culture' (occasionally 'alternative society') is seen as exhibiting a fundamental 'hostility to capitalism', and as generating, from the second decade of the century, a rejection of 'social, political and cultural norms', replacing them with 'a new behavioural pattern'. This culture, 'founded on class discipline, resourceful quasi-political illegality, direct action resulting often in guerrilla and open warfare, collectivist action of various forms, perverse humour and escapism', ultimately produced 'a society within a society', according to Francis and Smith. Whether this characterization can be sustained in its totality is open to serious doubt. Many aspects of miners' culture were not alternative, either in coalfield, Welsh or even British contexts. 'Respectability', religious observance, the popular press, the popularity of romantic novels and crime fiction, of the music hall and Hollywood films, of rugby union and association football: none of these can be considered 'alternative' pursuits, for they were part and parcel of working-class life in areas of Britain that enjoyed none of south Wales's reputation for militancy. Such a culture was not always approved, least of all by the Welsh intellectual élite, but neither was it conceived to be in deliberate opposition. In political terms the miners gave their support to a Labour Party that aimed to secure gradual change within the bounds of the law, rather than to the Communist Party which is most regularly highlighted as part of the 'alternative culture' and in the matter of trade-union behaviour and strike activity it is possible that this emphasis exaggerates 'radicalism' and 'militancy' at the expense of the continuity of patterns of leadership and representativeness, and the contingency of all industrial conflict.

As for 'proletarian internationalism', the culmination of many striking manifestations of such sentiment was the support, offered in the late 1930s, by the coalfield to the Republican cause in the Spanish Civil War. It is significant, however, that much more has been written on the relatively small numbers who volunteered to serve with the International Brigade than on the tens of thousands from mining communities who volunteered to fight on the Western Front during the First World War, for south Wales displayed some of the highest rates of recruitment in Britain during 1914 and 1915. This is not to counterpose 'patriotism' and 'internationalism', but it does suggest a rather more complex historical picture.

Whatever the specific criticisms, the sensitivity of *The Fed* to the complexity and integrity of its historical subjects, and its desire to comprehend that history from within, are qualities that merit continued respect and emulation, and since its publication most historians of the south Wales miners have sought to build on its achievement rather than seeking to construct a wholly different interpretation. Biographies of miners' leaders like Arthur Cook and S. O. Davies, studies of the miners of the anthracite coalfield, of industrial relations during the world wars, and of the South Wales Miners' Industrial Union have all enhanced our understanding of this society. Particularly important is the work of Ina-Maria Zweiniger-Bargielowska ('Miners' militancy', *Welsh History Review* (1992);

'South Wales miners' attitudes towards nationalisation', *Llafur* (1994)), who has challenged historical orthodoxy and what she views as the 'archetypal proletarian' stereotype embedded in it. In her writings south Wales miners appear far more passive, apolitical and prosaic in their concerns than they do in other histories, and although her work has not gone unchallenged (see, for instance, Bill Jones, Brian Roberts and Chris Williams, ' "Going from darkness to the light" ', *Llafur* (1996)), it has raised issues concerning historical perspective and the nature of historical evidence.

Comparative histories have also made their mark: David Gilbert, *Class, Community and Collective Action* (1992), brought together the polar opposites of the 1926 strike – the Nottinghamshire and south Wales miners – in a study of the relative importance of notions of 'class' and 'community' in the coalfields. Roger Fagge's *Power, Culture and Conflict in the Coalfields* (1996) goes further afield still with its transatlantic comparison between south Wales and West Virginia miners. Although not directly comparative, Huw Beynon and Terry Austrin's study of the Durham miners, *Masters and Servants* (1994), also yields many points of reference and contrast for scholars of south Wales, and Alan Campbell, Nina Fishman and David Howell (eds.), *Miners, Unions and Politics* (1996), intertwines the study of five British coalfields with more general thematic studies for the period 1910–47.

The political history of the coalfield has attracted nearly as much attention as have the miners' union and its struggles. Consistently in the limelight have been the exceptional aspects of south Walian politics when viewed in a British context: syndicalism, Communism and the strong tradition of independent working-class education that underpinned both. Bob Holton, *British Syndicalism* (1976), discusses syndicalist and 'proto-syndicalist' activity in south Wales before 1914, and Holton's interest, if not his conclusions, have been substantiated by David Egan and Keith Davies, amongst others. Although there is no study of the Communist Party itself, it figures prominently in Hywel Francis's *Miners Against Fascism* (1984) and Stuart Macintyre's *Little Moscows* (1980) and *A Proletarian Science* (1986). Richard Lewis, *Leaders and Teachers* (1993), is an outstanding history of the adult education movement in south Wales, undoubtedly one of the coalfield's distinctive social and ideological features, without which the strength and variety of the area's politics cannot be understood. Gradually, too, an appreciation of less exceptional aspects of political behaviour and choice has been emerging. Kenneth O. Morgan's enormous contribution to the political history of Wales has inevitably involved considerable treatment of the coalfield (see, in particular, his *Wales in British Politics* (1980), *Modern Wales: Politics, Places and People* (1995)). Deian Hopkin, Peter Stead and Jon Parry have all written on the labour movement up to 1914, and Chris Howard has produced incisive essays on the Labour Party in Aberavon. Chris Williams's *Democratic Rhondda* (1996) opens with the beginnings of labour representation in the area (in the 1880s), and explores Labour's growth, its domination of parliamentary and local representation in the inter-war years, and the strong challenge from the Communist Party. Finally, the works of Pyrs Gruffydd and Eddie May on housing reform and town and regional planning deserve recognition for their originality and insight. Major gaps remain: most significantly, a broad understanding of the Labour Party's electoral success and performance in local government is needed. The writing of the political history of the south Wales coalfield still, therefore, has some distance to go to provide a general understanding of fundamental aspects of that history, and there is need for detailed studies of the distinctive local politics of individual valleys.

The social history of the coalfield is, if anything, even less complete than its political history. The popular culture of coalfield society has received attention from David Smith and Gareth Williams (both, in *Fields of Praise* (1980); Smith, *Aneurin Bevan and the World of South Wales* (1993); Williams, *1905 and All That* (1991)), and Russell Davies's brilliant treatment of aspects of the social history of Carmarthenshire (*Secret Sins* (1996)) has much to offer on the problems and pressures of the developing western extremity of the coalfield. Migration flows (in both directions) and their social and linguistic consequences should yield fascinating scholarship for decades to come: for the purposes of this book the contributions of Colin Hughes (*Lime, Lemon and Sarsaparilla* (1991)) on the arrival of the Italians in Wales, and of Andy Chandler on out-migration from the Valleys to the prosperous industrial communities of the Midlands and the south of England are particularly relevant. The fortunes and status of the Welsh language in the coalfield have been examined in a preliminary way by scholars: the conclusions have been disparate and controversial, to say the least. As for religious practice and belief, the absence of any sustained treatment of this subject after the Religious

Revival of 1904–5 renders any summary of popular attitudes necessarily tentative, although Robert Pope, *Building Jerusalem* (1998), yields insights into the attempts of the Nonconformist churches to respond to the social problems in their midst.

Despite the trail-blazing efforts of a few historians, the greatest gap in the modern history of coalfield society is that of gender. Angela John (ed.), *Our Mothers' Land* (1991), stands alone as a book-length treatment of women in Welsh society. Deirdre Beddoe's essays have demonstrated how images of coalfield women do scant justice to the complexity and resourcefulness of their lives; Angela John has explored the contribution made by women to industrial protest; and Dot Jones has undertaken surveys of women's experiences of work and life expectancy. Rosemary Crook obtained first-hand testimonies from women in the Rhondda Valleys; Catherine Welsby has studied the fate of those bereaved by the Senghennydd disaster of 1913; and Neil Evans and Dot Jones have investigated the campaign for pit-head baths in the coalfield. Sheila Owen-Jones has considered women in the tinplate industry, and Mari Williams's work on women in Royal Ordnance Factories during the Second World War has much to offer on a broader front (see *'Where is Mrs Jones Going?'* (1995)). All of these works are underpinned by the written testimonies collected in Carol White and Siân Rhiannon Williams (eds.), *Struggle or Starve* (1998), and Leigh Verrill-Rhys and Deirdre Beddoe (eds.), *Parachutes and Petticoats* (1992). Nevertheless, efforts to comprehend family dynamics, and the construction of concepts of femininity and masculinity in coalfield society remain fragmented or incipient. Very little has been written on female experiences of domestic service or on women in teaching, generally the only professional career open to women in the coalfield. Women's involvement in political activity (such as the Co-operative Women's Guild), limited though it might have been by prevailing assumptions and family pressures, also demands a more sustained investigation. If the economic dimension to coalfield history deserves greater integration into the mainstream of coalfield histories, so do considerations of gender if our histories are not to remain lopsided.

Few historians have attempted to draw all threads of society together in one volume. The *Glamorgan County History* attempts such a synthesis in two (volume V, noted above, and volume VI, *Glamorgan Society*, edited by Prys Morgan (1988)); but Michael Lieven's *Senghennydd: The Universal Pit Village* (1994) is truly exceptional in the way in which it addresses economic and social development, two terrible pit disasters and their consequences, politics, trade union-ism, popular culture and, significantly, the histories of women, children and families. More works of such scope are desperately needed. In the absence of 'complete' social history, only the best of autobiographies can at the present substitute: Wil Jon Edwards, *From the Valley I Came* (1956), offers numerous insights, though it does not rival the profound achievement of Bert Coombes's *These Poor Hands* (1939). [**DOCUMENT I**]

The question of the relationship of the literature of the coalfield to its history is vast, and the potential of the former for an under-standing of the latter is still only partly appreciated. There are more beginnings than endings, but James A. Davies (ed.), *The Heart of Wales* (1994), and Meic Stephens (ed.), *A Rhondda Anthology* (1993), open some doors. One novelist who offers a sweeping history of the coalfield in a chronology substantially equivalent to that of this work is Lewis Jones: see his *Cwmardy* (1937) and *We Live* (1939).

Surveying what was then but a modest achievement, in 1975 David Smith summarized the challenge for future historians of the south Wales coalfield ('The future of coalfield history', 62–3):

> History emerges when we bridge the gap between a past living actuality and our present fragmented evidence by reconstructing the plethora of detail in language. The future of coalfield history must then, also be about our imaginative repossession of the past. Somehow there must be an objective analysis bolstered by statistics and documentation that can also convey what it was like to stand in drizzling rain in Kenfig Hill in 1928, waiting amongst bankrupt boarded-up shops for an infrequent, stuttering bus; how peeling, green-distempered Institute walls smelled; what it meant to buy spectacles from a job-lot in a Penny Bazaar by a squinting process of trial and error, and how good a day out at the vulgar gimcrack seaside was after years of being hemmed in by brown-varnished houses and black tarpapered sheds.

It is salutary that much of the agenda that Smith set out in 1975 remains unaddressed. The south Wales coalfield continues to offer its historians manifold tasks: to capture the strategic and tactical decision-making processes of the coalowner, trade union and political party alongside sexual desire, escapism, family pressures, household dynamics, generational tensions, individual and collective aspirations, religious faith and a sense of human morality. There needs to be more integration of the histories of businesses and the histories of the workers they employed, more on the human impact of major events such as wars, and a greater sense of how individuals made careers and life-style choices, and shaped the world into which their children were born. Ultimately, it is the responsibility of the historian to produce histories that people might have lived, in which readers may recognize themselves and their ancestors. As we enter the twenty-first century, the south Wales coalfield may be almost wholly consigned to the past, and the miners become virtually extinct as an industrial and political force of any contemporary weight; but the study of this unique, rich society remains, if not in its infancy, then most certainly still in its adolescence, and it is a study that, like adolescence itself, offers great scope for impassioned debate.

2. The Rise and Fall of the South Wales Coalfield

During the second half of the nineteenth century, the south Wales coal industry expanded rapidly. Great strides were made in the exploitation of the area's reserves of steam coal (48 per cent of total reserves), which was particularly suitable for raising steam in boilers and which found its greatest application in marine engines. Of the other types of coal, bituminous coal (30 per cent of total reserves) was more appropriate to household purposes and was often termed 'house' coal, whilst the anthracite coal (22 per cent) found in the west of the coalfield was eventually matched to specialized stoves. Following pioneering developments in the Cynon Valley in the late 1830s and 1840s, steam-coal measures began to be worked in the Rhondda Fawr from the mid-1850s. Whereas, in 1854, 8.5m tons of coal were being mined annually in south Wales, twenty years later the total had doubled to 16.5m tons, 26 per cent of which was exported, and the industry employed 73,000 miners. These figures represented some 13 per cent of the total British output of coal, and 14 per cent of the total British work-force in the industry. Expansion continued until the end of the century with hitherto largely untouched valleys being exploited (the Ogwr Fach and Fawr in the 1860s, the Garw in the 1870s, the Aber in the 1890s). By the eve of the coal dispute of 1898, production had risen to 36m tons annually, and employment to 127,000 (18 per cent of both British output and work-force). South Wales was by this stage predominantly an exporting coalfield, with 20m tons (56 per cent of its production) destined for overseas markets, and its huge expansion had been fuelled by massive in-migration of labour from Wales and, to a lesser extent at this stage, from the west of England. [**DOCUMENT II**] Mining, although a harsh and highly dangerous occupation, was, in comparison with other manual jobs, well rewarded when employment was regular: average earnings for south Wales miners in 1891 were 6s. 6d. per shift, twice the rate of pay for agricultural workers in Glamorgan.

Sporadic attempts to organize miners in some form of recognizable trade-union organization had been made since the 1840s, but most bodies had only a transient existence. The Amalgamated Association of Mineworkers (AAM) had, between 1869 and 1875, represented the strongest of such attempts, but it had been crushed following three industrial disputes of considerable scale and bitterness. The AAM and the strife of the early 1870s had been succeeded by the Sliding Scale system of wage regulation, by which miners' wages were automatically linked to the selling price of coal. The coalfield-wide scope of the AAM had been replaced by fragmented local union structures based on individual valleys or areas, such as the Neath, Swansea and Llanelly Miners' Association and the Monmouthshire District Miners' Association. Geography reinforced localism, as did the divisions in the coal market between domestic and export-bound coals, and between bituminous and steam coals. In the Rhondda Valleys, the Cambrian Miners' Association faced in 1888 the establishment of a separate Rhondda Valley House Coal Miners' Association as a result of such divisions. In the Garw Valley, the Garw Miners' Association was characterized by a division of interests between the four steam-coal pits in the upper valley, and a host of smaller house-coal levels lower down and in the plain between the River Garw and Bridgend. Within the mining work-force, hewers on piece-rates and hauliers or surfacemen on day-rates could find their interests diverging, the clearest expression of this being in the 1893 'Hauliers' or 'Rocking-Stone' strike, when marching gangs of hauliers striking for a 20 per cent wage increase brought out miners across the coalfield. Ironstone miners represented an additional threat to unity amongst colliers, for they were usually paid at lower rates and were willing to take the places of others involved in industrial action. In a rapidly growing society, ethnic tension also occasionally reared its head: the AAM found its support weakened by accusations that it was insufficiently 'Welsh' in character, and by the attempt to establish a Welsh-speaking alternative union, whilst Irish workers could also find themselves on the receiving end of indigenous hostility, as occurred at Tredegar in 1882. The facts of high labour turnover and fluid settlement patterns in the industrial areas only exacerbated the difficulties and inhibited the growth of a strong trade unionism.

Atop the uneven pyramid of local or market-specific union bodies sat the workmen's representatives on the Joint Sliding Scale Committee. Their leader was the Rhondda-based William Abraham, also known by his bardic name, Mabon, who had served in office with the AAM in Loughor before coming to the Rhondda in 1877. Having witnessed the destruction of one trade union, Mabon was keen to avoid repeating the experience, and placed great emphasis on maintaining an atmosphere of unity and harmony of interests between employers and employees in the coal trade. This policy enabled the miners to have a permanent place in the counsels of the powerful, but the very nature of the Sliding Scale ensured that any control of their own standard of living was out of the miners' hands, and instead at the mercy of the vagaries of demand and the levels of production. Furthermore, the Sliding Scale implied a permanent upper limit to the relative level of remuneration which the miners would receive for their efforts. Discontent with the system grew gradually, spread in part through such lodges of the Mineworkers' Federation of Great Britain (MFGB) that were established in Monmouthshire from the end of the 1880s onwards, and that found their local spokesman in the person of Risca miners' leader, William Brace. Opposition was most clearly expressed in the 1893 strike, although this failed to attract the widespread support that would have been necessary for a full-scale assault on the Sliding Scale principle.

The colliery owners, as well as the miners, realized that they could benefit from collective organization, and formed first the Aberdare Steam Collieries Association in 1864, and then, in 1873, the Monmouthshire and South Wales Collieries Association (from 1890 named the Monmouthshire and South Wales Coal Owners' Association – MSWCOA). Although many coalowners remained outside this organization, and it functioned less as a means of economic self-regulation than as a mechanism by which conflicts with the men might be pursued more successfully, by the mid-1880s its members were producing about half of the coalfield's output, and from the end of the nineteenth century this rose to around 80 per cent.

The coalowners pursued an aggressive, uncompromising policy during the dispute of 1898, which lasted from April until September, and which resulted in their almost total victory. The dispute centred on an attempt by the miners to arrive at a new Sliding Scale agreement on more favourable terms: the end-product was little change, and the ending of the custom of Mabon's day, the miners' monthly holiday. Yet, as Ness Edwards wrote, 'Though this struggle ended in defeat it was the fire which knit together the miners into the South Wales Miners' Federation' (*History of the SWMF*, 2). Convinced, at last, of the necessity of coalfield-wide organization to match the employers in extent and strength, the SWMF was founded on 25 October 1898. Although Mabon's conduct of the negotiations during the dispute had been subjected to severe criticism, he was retained as SWMF president (and held that office until 1912). But his beloved Sliding Scale was condemned as the 'Fed' committed itself to the severing of the link between prices and wages and the replacement of the Joint Sliding Scale Committee by a Conciliation Board. In 1899 the Fed affiliated to the MFGB, having already enlisted 60,000 members, and by the end of 1900 it claimed 127,894 members, representing 87 per cent of the total work-force employed in the south Wales coal industry. [**DOCUMENT III**]

The catharsis of 1898 over, the coal industry returned to a period of intense growth. New collieries, such as the Britannia and Penallta in the Rhymney Valley, the Lady Lewis and Ferndale No.9 in the Rhondda Fach, Coedely in the Ely Valley and St John's in the Llynfi, continued to be established through to the First World War. Production broke through the 40m-ton barrier in 1902, and passed 50m tons in 1908, 62 per cent of which was destined for export markets. The work-force continued to grow in tandem: numbering 150,000 in 1901, it had reached 201,000 by 1908.

Beneath the combined images of industrial prosperity, political unity and social progress were concealed some rather more worrying truths. Although the long-term decline in labour productivity from the 1880s onwards was as much a reflection of the almost unreal expansion of that decade as it was of the structural problems facing coal entrepreneurs, colliery profits were being squeezed in the first decade of the twentieth century, and, given the high prices already asked for Welsh coal on the international market, passing on costs in the form of price rises was not an option. The introduction of the 1908 Eight Hours Act (limiting coal-winding time to eight hours in a shift and bringing the length of the average day underground in south Wales down from 9.75 to 8.75 hours) led to a step down in productivity and thus in profits for the employers, and it also depressed the earning potential of hewers, whose wages were determined by piece-rates and who thus had, following the Act, fewer hours in which to earn the same level of pay. Another legal change that aggravated miners' discontents was the decision of Judge Roberts in 1908 that compensatory allowances for colliers working in difficult, less productive seams ('abnormal places') were a matter of custom (and therefore revocable by employers) rather than of law.

Compounding these fundamental difficulties was an imperfect Conciliation Board structure, whose lengthy arbitration procedures were often inconclusive, leading to frustration on both sides of the labour/capital equation.

Within the coalowners' camp, differences of opinion and personality clashes, especially between Sir William Thomas Lewis (until 1903 chairman of the Coalowners' Association) and D. A. Thomas (owner of the Cambrian Collieries) were not unknown, but they were as nothing in comparison with the tensions building within the SWMF itself. Towards the end of the first decade of the new century, the policy of compromise that Mabon personified had to face the criticisms not only of the advocates (such as James Winstone of Risca) of a more confrontational industrial and political policy, but also the scorn of the flamboyant 'young man in a hurry', Charles Stanton, miners' agent for Aberdare, who castigated 'the faint-hearted, over-cautious, creeping, crawling, cowardly set who pose as leaders but do not lead [and] are responsible for the rotten condition of things today'. As a result of all these problems, south Wales was marked by a high level of industrial unrest, especially in the mining and quarrying sector of the economy, even before the years 1910–14 which are commonly labelled those of the 'Great' or 'Labour Unrest'. Across the period 1901–13, Welsh workers in that sector were five-and-a-half times more strike-prone than the British average for all workers, and 70 per cent more strike-prone than the British average for workers in the same sector.

Politically, Wales, certainly from the General Election of 1868 onwards, had been a stronghold of Liberal Party support, and such labour leaders as came to the fore had, almost without exception, aligned themselves with the party and its avowed primary goal of disestablishment. Thus Mabon, MP for the Rhondda constituency from its formation in 1885 until his retirement from Parliament in 1920, acted out a thoroughly conventional political role as a 'Lib-Lab' for most of his years, and he was followed in the twentieth century by colleagues Thomas Richards (secretary of the SWMF and MP for West Monmouthshire, 1904–18), William Brace (vice-president of the SWMF and president 1912–15, and MP for South Glamorgan, 1906–18), and John Williams (miners' agent for the SWMF's Western District and MP for the Gower constituency, 1906–22). The degree of unity between these labour leaders and the overwhelmingly middle-class Liberal associations that backed them should not be overstated: in each case either their nomination as a

Liberal candidate or their eventual victory as a Lib-Lab MP had been achieved in the teeth of opposition, either from within the Liberal Party itself, or in the form of a rival (sometimes official) Liberal candidate. Through, at the very least, their electoral success, each made an important contribution to raising the profile of the labour movement in Wales, but none of the four 'Lib-Lab' MPs had much sympathy with either the Independent Labour Party (ILP), the Labour Representation Committee (from 1906 the Labour Party) or with socialism in general. Mabon, in fact, was an active campaigner against the proposal to affiliate the MFGB to the Labour Party, which eventually became reality in 1909, converting him and his fellow Lib-Labs into Labour MPs (in name at least) overnight. As the first decade of the twentieth century progressed, they appeared more and more to be on the defensive. Keir Hardie, elected MP for Merthyr Boroughs in 1900 following his vigorous campaigning on behalf of the miners in 1898, spoke with greater passion on their behalf in the Commons than did any of the Lib-Labs. ILP branches spread across the coalfield, sporadically and temporarily during 1898, but taking firmer root from around 1904 onwards and attracting the sympathies of many younger miners. Coalfield products such as T. I. Mardy Jones and Noah Ablett were heavily involved in the developing adult-education movement of the new century, as Welsh miners attended Ruskin College and then returned to run evening classes for those of their comrades who were interested. Gradually a much stronger and uncompromising critique of capitalism than was available from the mouths of the Lib-Labs was articulated, and an aggressive class consciousness permeated the minds of many, if not all, miners.

All these trends, in the economy, industrial relations, trade union and party politics of the south Wales coalfield, can be seen to culminate in the years 1910–12. Three industrial disputes stand out: the Cambrian Combine dispute of 1910–11, the Cynon Valley dispute of 1910 and the participation of the south Wales miners in the first national strike of the British miners, for a minimum wage, in 1912. Taken together, these momentous events heralded the emergence of the south Wales coalfield as a 'storm centre' of industrial unrest.

The Cambrian Combine dispute was remarkable for four characteristics. It encompassed approximately 11,000 men distributed between four separate collieries (three in Mid-Rhondda, one in the Ogwr Fach), but all under the control of one coalowner: the

autocratic D. A. Thomas. The conflict took the form of a clash
between the Cambrian Combine, the epitome of capitalist combination and progressiveness, and a men's combine committee, organized
to meet the scale of the challenge, and led by a new generation who
were, if not all syndicalists, at least cognizant of the advanced views
now in circulation. [**DOCUMENT IV**] Secondly, in running from
September 1910 to August 1911, the dispute lasted longer than any
major strike in living memory. Thirdly, it involved large-scale and
persistent violence not only during the Tonypandy Riots of
November 1910 (which occasioned the notorious importation of the
military into the district) but for months thereafter. Finally, it
inspired the 'advanced men' of the SWMF to produce a thorough
critique of the existing personnel and traditions of their union, in the
process drawing upon syndicalist and industrial unionist theory. This
was embodied in the publication of the Unofficial Reform Committee, *The Miners' Next Step*. [**DOCUMENT V**]

Starting some weeks after and finishing many months before the
Cambrian Combine dispute, the strike of the 11,000 miners of the
Aberdare district merged into that of its Rhondda and Gilfach
neighbours in the contemporary and official mind. Yet in origin and
course it was quite distinct, representing the culmination of many
months of tension in the Cynon Valley between the miners, led by
their agent, Charles Stanton, and the major employer in the area, the
Powell Duffryn Coal Company. The occasion for the dispute was the
company's termination of the custom by which the men could take
home waste wood for firewood. The men's response was to 'down
tools' and to bring out on strike other pits in the valley by marching
to the pit-heads and exhorting miners there to join what was an
'unofficial' strike. Sensational rhetoric was common on both sides,
and troops also arrived in the Cynon Valley, with violent clashes there
also between strikers and police. Financial hardship gradually
impelled the Aberdare men to seek a resolution of the dispute, and
this was achieved, with no gain for the men, in January 1911. Martin
Barclay has written that the strike's importance lies in its similarity
with the 'Tonypandy experience . . . [which] shows that, far from
being a freak or a conspiracy, the upheavals that took place were the
product of a process of social and industrial change which went on to
engulf the whole coalfield and shape its post-war history' (' "The
Slaves of the Lamp" ', 36).

In critical respects the struggles of the south Wales miners during
1910–11 prepared the ground for the national strike of 1912. The

issue of 'abnormal places' and that of its essential corollary, the minimum wage, had been widely publicized and taken on as a primary objective by the MFGB. As for the strike itself, although not a complete success (the level of the minimum wage secured was much lower than that initially demanded), according to Ness Edwards, 'It welded the miners of Great Britain, for the first time, into a solid fighting force, and made national action a reality' (*The History of the SWMF*, 50).

Both the peaceful, progressive image of Liberal Wales and the bounteous rhetoric of coal-trade harmony were laid to rest by the events of 1910–12. 'Lib-Lab' notions of industrial co-operation had been exposed as wishful by the stark opposition of labour and capital manifested in the disputes of these years. If Mabon's motto had been 'half a loaf is better than none', Ruskin College product, Cambrian Combine Committee Vice-Chairman and co-author of *The Miners' Next Step*, Noah Rees, could pithily respond that '[w]e are demanding the bakehouse'. Of even greater significance was the realization that the object of industrial struggle was henceforth not simply an improved relationship between wages and profits but the determination of both the leadership and the future trajectory of coalfield society as a whole.

These were battles started, not battles won: radical ideas had to be maintained outside the context of specific industrial disputes, and advanced by initially unfamiliar spokesmen who did not have the benefit of either a mouthpiece in the press, or support from journalists and editors themselves, who were quick to recognize that old allegiances would no longer apply. The degree of influence that syndicalist and industrial unionist leaders possessed should not be overstated: most representative positions in the SWMF continued to be held by men who preferred the more predictable (and perhaps no less efficacious) routines of conciliation to the weapon of the unofficial strike or the rhetoric of class warfare. Syndicalist-inspired schemes for the centralization of the SWMF were clearly defeated in 1912 and 1913, and politically the tenor of the union remained constitutional, not revolutionary.

This last dimension represented nothing less than an appreciation of electoral reality. A notable contrast of the years immediately preceding the First World War is that between the miners' avowed militancy, and the run of defeats suffered by Labour candidates (excepting the 'Lib-Labs') at parliamentary elections in mining constituencies. In 1910, Vernon Hartshorn, miners' agent for the Maesteg District, failed twice to win the Mid-Glamorgan seat against

Liberal opposition, whilst Charles Stanton was defeated in East Glamorgan. J. H. Williams was twice defeated, in 1910 and 1912, in East Carmarthenshire. Part of the explanation is to be found in the fact that, given exclusions under the franchise, not all miners had parliamentary votes to cast, and younger miners in particular may have been disfranchised. Additionally, although the miners were predominant in many constituencies, other workers did not necessarily share their political and industrial opinions, and could prefer a traditional middle-class Liberal representative in parliament to someone usually portrayed as a 'hothead' and 'firebrand' by the local press, even if he was a fellow worker. Finally, with no general election being held after December 1910, it is difficult to be certain as to the likely level of support for Labour candidates in the wake of the 'Labour Unrest'. Although Labour had begun to make significant progress on certain local government bodies before the First World War (in Rhondda and Merthyr in particular), it would have to await the reformed franchise and changed conditions in post-war Britain in order to make a major political breakthrough. [**DOCUMENT VI**]

Despite the disputatious nature of these pre-war years, the south Wales coal industry continued to set new records. Peak production figures were reached in 1913 (57m tons), and Professor Stanley Jevons could predict that the coalfield would continue to yield up to 100m tons per annum for at least 200 years. The war itself created a great demand for coal. The Admiralty, which previously had an annual order for 1.5m tons of south Wales steam coal, increased its purchasing to 15m tons. Coal was in great demand at munitions factories, and in iron, steel and tinplate works and foundries. Colliery company profits rose, and the miners demanded wage increases commensurate both with these profits and the rising cost of living. When the coalowners proved resistant, the result was a coalfield-wide strike.

Subject at the time to misrepresentation ('German bribery'), the strike of July 1915 (in which south Wales miners flouted both the Munitions Act and the instructions of their own Executive Council) has also been the victim of historians' misinterpretations. The view that it was the result of an 'excess of patriotism' on the part of the south Wales miners is highly exaggerated, but then so is the argument that it represented an 'anti-war feeling', 'unconscious' or otherwise. More accurate is J. Vyrnwy Morgan's observation that

> the circumstances of the war intensified the men's convictions that
> they were being exploited by their employers and by the Government.

They believed that they were morally and legally entitled to a share in the boom of prosperity which, as they alleged, the war had brought to their employers.[1]

It was the material interests and grievances of the miners that lay at the root of their actions in 1915, and which prompted David Lloyd George to hurry down to Cardiff to pacify them.

The critical importance of the coal industry to the war effort led to the state taking a steadily rising interest in the management of production and of industrial relations. Initially this took the form of export licensing, but, from December 1916, a coal controller was appointed who had responsibility for profit regulation and the supervision of wage negotiations. Also in 1916 the SWMF secured an agreement from the coalowners that all colliery workmen should be members of one of the recognized trade unions: this assisted in extinguishing the curse of non-unionism whilst also strengthening the central position of the SWMF itself: henceforward, the appropriate home in the mining industry for all except enginemen, craftsmen and colliery officials.

Of more immediate importance were the improvements secured in pay that saw average money earnings more than double between 1914 and 1918, and the gathering of support for the realization of the MFGB's objective of the permanent nationalization of the mines, based on a belief that the miners had a right to a higher standard of living, and to special treatment by state and nation. [**DOCUMENT VII**] The war years, although not introducing wholly novel vistas of ambition on the part of the miners, helped to generalize, popularize and confirm the combativeness of the years 1910–12.

The 'home front' was only one part of the experience of war undergone by coalfield society as a whole. Precise recruitment figures for the south Wales area do not exist, but there was widespread initial enthusiasm for soldiering amongst miners, headed by some prominent labour leaders including Mabon, David Watts Morgan and Frank Hodges. In Glamorgan nearly 50,000 men volunteered for Kitchener's New Army by May 1915, and miners formed the bulk of the 1st and 2nd Rhondda Pals battalions of the Welsh Regiment and of the 1st and 2nd Gwents of the South Wales Borderers. Charles Stanton, the Cynon Valley demagogue, switched from revolutionary to jingoistic rhetoric, and won the Merthyr Boroughs seat following Keir Hardie's death in 1915, against the official SWMF candidate, James Winstone. Up to a quarter of the

MFGB's membership was believed to have enlisted by mid-1915, with Glamorgan being amongst the areas with the highest recruiting rates. The anti-war movement, by contrast, was minuscule and fragmented between revolutionary socialists, syndicalists and Christian pacifists. Popular resentment of wartime conditions appeared largely in the form of discontent with food shortages, high rents and prices, reports of profiteering and disillusionment with the seemingly relentless slaughter on the Western Front.

In the aftermath of the war, south Wales miners continued to benefit from the circumstances offered by the continuation of government control and the upsurge of a post-war boom. Employment in the coalfield rose to an all-time high of 271,516 in 1920, and average money earnings were more than treble those of 1914. Miners' leaders believed that the nationalization of the industry was an idea whose time had very much arrived, but after the initial wave of public sympathy during the first stage of the Sankey Commission's deliberations had led to an increase in wages and a cut in hours, the momentum for public ownership slumped amongst miners as well as more widely. Despite the fact that the majority of the reports issued by the commission recommended nationalization, their predictable diversity (the commission being split between workers' and employers' interests) allowed the government to refuse to consider this option any further. Strategically, the MFGB had been outmanœuvred by the wily Welshman at No. 10 Downing Street.

The immediate post-war prosperity was as temporary and fragile as the MFGB's ability to keep the pressure on Lloyd George. Labour productivity had fallen by a quarter between 1914 and 1920; and with the collapse of the export price of coal at the end of 1920, resulting in south Wales coal being produced at a loss of 6s. per ton by the beginning of 1921, it was hardly surprising that the government seized the earliest opportunity to return the troublesome industry to private control in April 1921. This was again the occasion for a major strike. The miners, initially backed by the other partners in the Triple Alliance (the National Union of Railwaymen and the Transport and General Workers' Union), wanted to see the establishment of a nationally based wages settlement system that would unify districts (irrespective of the market for which the bulk of their coal output was destined). To the coalowners such an outcome would have restricted their ability to cut wages, and would have maintained a question mark over the long-term future of private ownership of the mines. The miners struck from April to July, but the promised support of the other Triple Alliance unions did not materialize, and a return to work on the terms offered was the result. In south Wales the consequences of defeat were severe, and average money earnings halved in the course of 1921. Initially, this seemed to have beneficial consequences, at least for the coal industry as a whole: there was something of a trade recovery from 1922 to 1924 as production topped 54m tons in 1923, and employment stabilized at around a quarter of a million. But this was as much the result of international events as it was of any fundamental resolution of the problems of the industry: in 1922 an American coal strike boosted British exports to the USA and to markets normally served by American coal exporters, and in 1923 the French occupation of the Ruhr coalfield led to the loss of German coal exports, a major competitor in European markets. By the end of 1924, however, both German and American competition had returned in full force, and costs and unemployment rose. Another confrontation between coalowners and miners seemed unavoidable. [**DOCUMENT VIII**]

Although industrially beleaguered in the early 1920s, the south Wales miners nevertheless managed to generate strong political representation. At the 'Khaki' election held in December 1918 their advances were somewhat limited by the presence of Coalition candidates who frequently united Conservative and Liberal support, and by the mood of popular relief and appreciation for Lloyd George. Labour candidates who had given any reason to be thought 'anti-war', such as the Revd T. E. Nicholas in Aberdare, fared badly. But Labour did take nine seats across the coalfield, averaging 47 per cent of the vote in contested elections, and the following spring took control of both Glamorgan and Monmouthshire County Councils, as well as a clutch of Urban District Councils. The Liberal opposition collapsed before the next general election, in 1922, and on this occasion Labour took eighteen seats in Wales, including all those that can be designated as 'coalfield' seats (and increasing its share of the vote to 55 per cent). Sitting for Aberavon from 1922 to 1929 was Ramsay MacDonald, the leader of the Labour Party and, in 1924, its first prime minister. But Labour's studied avoidance of any endorsement of industrial action, allied to its minority status, meant that no resolution of the coal industry's difficulties emerged from that quarter, and before 1924 was over the Conservatives were back in power.

1925 was a tense year in the political economy of coal. The return to the Gold Standard in April 1925 damaged exports, and the

Mining Association of Great Britain (the employers' organization) announced wide-ranging wage cuts on a district basis from 31 July, supplemented by a return to the eight-hour day. The Baldwin government intervened to stave off the crisis with a £10m subsidy that lasted to May 1926, but without a trade revival, and with both sides adopting increasingly entrenched positions, a full-scale confrontation appeared inevitable. The additional dimension to the clash of 1926 was the involvement of the TUC General Council. This resulted in the General Strike, and nine days of largely successful solidarity between industrial workers. But the General Council were not prepared to handle the political imperatives of extra-parliamentary direct action: they had been playing industrial-relations brinkmanship, not planning a full-scale revolution. After the collapse of the General Strike, the miners fought on alone until the end of November and eventual defeat.

After 1926 the south Wales miners had to accept that their fight for a reasonable standard of living had been lost, at least in the medium term. The revolutionaries of the coalfield had to shelve their ambitious projects and face up to living in an undeniably non-revolutionary age. A substantial shift of power took place, away from the miners and towards the coalowners. Union and political activists were subjected to widespread victimization, wages were cut, hours extended, and working conditions deteriorated. Employment in the coal industry fell steadily from 1926 to 1937 (from 218,00 to 136,000), and by 1932 male unemployment across Wales as a whole was averaging 39 per cent. The SWMF, reacting slowly to the changed circumstances in which it had to operate, found itself regarded by some miners as powerless to defend their interests, and blamed by others for the disasters that had befallen them and their society. Non-unionism, encouraged by some employers, became rife, some workers were attracted by other unions, and the South Wales Miners' Industrial Union (MIU), an explicitly 'non-political' organization founded in 1926, plagued the Fed for more than a decade before its extinction in 1938.

The slow rebuilding of the SWMF in the face of the threat of the MIU and more general employer hostility was one facet of a many-sided politicization of the coalfield in the late 1920s and 1930s. The spectres of unemployment, poverty, malnutrition and disease occasioned national hunger marches, localized campaigns (often spearheaded by the National Unemployed Workers' Movement) and vast, spectacular and successful demonstrations against the Means

Test in 1935. South Wales may have been a society in crisis, but it still had time to place its harrowing experiences in an international context. In response to the spread of Fascism in Germany and Italy, the outbreak of the Spanish Civil War in 1936 gave rise to widespread support for the Republican regime. This involved the collection of food, the giving of aid, the reception of refugees, the holding of meetings and rallies; and, most famously, south Wales supplied 134 volunteers to the International Brigade, thirty-three of whom died in the conflict. The Communist Party was to the fore in many of these campaigns against oppression at home and abroad, but in terms of political representation and the regular allegiances of the majority of miners and their families it remained a long way behind Labour. No Communist was ever returned for a parliamentary constituency in the coalfield, and the party made a significant impression on only a few local government bodies. Labour instead continued to exercise almost total dominance of politics in the region: it held the fifteen coalfield seats without interruption, even during the national disaster of the 1931 general election, and gradually took control of more and more local authorities. [**DOCUMENT IX**] As the 1930s drew to a close, the SWMF was back in control of its members, and if not on wholly secure ground in its dealings with employers (in what remained an uncertain economic climate), nevertheless it could look to the future and concentrate on improving wages and conditions, rather than on mere survival in the face of orchestrated hostility. The 1937 Wages Agreement was evidence of the new, disciplined approach to industrial relations being pioneered by SWMF president, Arthur Horner.

The outbreak of the Second World War initially had a positive impact on the coal industry. Rearmament and the exigencies of the war economy resulted in an increased demand for coal and its workers, leading to an easing of unemployment and a rise in wages. The fall of France in May/June 1940 brought this brief prosperity to an abrupt end. The export market collapsed and many collieries closed. Production fell from 35m tons in 1939 to 22m tons in 1944, and the work-force fell by over 16,000. In industrial relations, the mood of the 1930s remained influential, in spite of the extremities of the conflict with Germany. The deep embitterment of the miners could not be swept away overnight, and a high level of unofficial strikes resulted. The conviction grew that private ownership of the industry was damaging not just to the miners' standard of living, but also to the efficiency and flexibility of the industry itself. From midway through the war reconstruction became a prominent theme in the leadership circles of the Welsh Labour movement, and nationalization of coal was centrally embedded in any proposals that resulted. Labour's sweeping victory in the General Election of 1945 was followed in 1946 by the Coal Industry Nationalization Bill, and those many mining trade unionists who had sacrificed time, effort, earnings and even civil liberty to fight for their union and their class believed that coal nationalization was a major step on the road to a new Britain. [**DOCUMENT X**]

The coal industry that began the nationalized era was very different from that which had struggled through the inter-war decades. The number of working pits had been drastically pruned, from nearly 500 in the 1920s to 222, and output, at 21m tons in 1947, was far below the 35m of 1939. This rose slightly to a peak of 24m tons in 1952, and was sustained throughout the remainder of the decade, in spite of seventy-four pit closures between 1947 and 1960. In the 1960s production dropped first to around 19m tons, and then down further to 13m in 1970. At this point there were still over fifty working collieries in the coalfield. Employment, which had stood at 115,500 at nationalization, fell below 100,000 in 1959 and below 50,000 a decade later.

As a result of this gradual rationalization, the historic reliance of the south Wales economy on the coal industry was eased somewhat. The cruel lessons of too great a dependence on one generator of wealth had been learnt, and a sustained effort was made to broaden the economic base of south Wales, and to develop an indigenous manufacturing sector. This had some success, with the revival of the steel industry, the conversion of the wartime Royal Ordnance Factories to trading estates, and the introduction of government-assisted factories, but talk of a 'second industrial revolution' was over-optimistic, and growth was more rapid in the service sector by the 1960s.

The limited impact of the economic reconstruction of south Wales, and the failure to generate substantial job opportunities that might have compensated for the level of redundancy in the coal industry, placed a new meaning on the latent industrial relations troubles in the mines. At the outset of nationalization, the south Wales miners had enjoyed a brief period of industrial relations quiescence, and were responsible for proportionally less loss of output through disputes than most other British coalfields until the beginning of the 1950s. However, with very few exceptions, from 1951 onwards the south Wales miners restored their reputation for industrial militancy. In 1966 south Wales, which produced less than a tenth of total British output, was nevertheless responsible for over half of the total output lost through industrial disputes. The discontent that was building throughout the 1950s and 1960s culminated in the clashes between the NUM and the Conservative government led by Edward Heath in 1972 and 1974. In effect these represented the last gasp of an aggressive mining militancy, and did nothing to address the very real problem of deindustrialization in the coalfield, and the economic marginalization of former colliery settlements. After an inconclusive squaring-up between the NUM and the new Conservative government in 1980, the latter, with the connivance of the National Coal Board, sought a head-on confrontation with the miners in 1984. Possibly deluded by historical mythology, and certainly over-confident, the union leadership accepted battle on the worst possible terrain. After more than a year of struggle, in which the resourcefulness, courage and doggedness of union members and their families shamed both the foolhardiness of their leaders and the naked vindictiveness of the state, the miners were defeated. The consequences for many British coalfields were disastrous, none more so than south Wales. On the eve of the strike, 20,000 miners had been employed in the twenty-eight mines of south Wales, producing 7m tons of coal. A decade later British Coal attempted to close the last deep mine in the coalfield at Tower Colliery, Hirwaun. In a symbolic act, Tower was instead the subject of a successful buy-out operation by its own employees (over 200 strong), who established ownership in January 1995. Whatever its long-term future, Tower Colliery symbolizes for now a dual reconciliation of the forces of labour and capital, which were so long opposed, and of south Wales society with the industry that gave it birth.

good conclusion

3.   The Industry

During the half-century covered by this book, the south Wales coalfield probably came as close to being a 'mono-industrial society' as was or is possible in an industrialized country. 'Coal' was 'King', and this was a monarch whose predominance left no space for any pretenders to the throne. The 1921 census recorded that of the 574,553 occupied males of twelve years of age and above in the counties of Glamorgan and Monmouthshire, no fewer than 225,437 were employed in the mining and quarrying sector, a remarkable 39 per cent of the whole. A closer examination of the coalfield at this time reveals a much greater dependence of employment on this single industry. In the Rhondda Urban District there were no fewer than 41,508 coal miners, representing 74 per cent of the male workforce. Similar percentages (of over 70 per cent) could be found in the Ogmore and Garw, Maesteg, Glyncorrwg, and Mountain Ash Urban Districts in Glamorgan, and in the Nantyglo and Blaina, Mynyddislwyn, Abertillery, Rhymney and Abercarn Urban Districts in Monmouthshire. A further eight Glamorgan, six Monmouthshire and two Carmarthenshire local authority areas had over half their male workers in the mines. The onset of difficult times in the industry in the 1920s led to a slight diminution in the industry's domination, but at the 1931 census mining and quarrying still accounted for over a third of all male workers in Glamorgan and Monmouthshire, and it was not until the 1951 census that the proportion fell below one-fifth.

As signified by these dramatic statistics, the coalfield's economy was heavily reliant on this one industry. Even in those areas where other industries (such as steel and tinplate) had a presence, coal-mining remained the major employer (47 per cent of all workers in the Ebbw Vale Urban District as opposed to 16 per cent in the metal trades, for instance). Many other workers, in the transport sector, in brickworks, quarries, coal carbonization plants and breweries, were dependent on the orders of the coal industry and its employees. At times most of this coal was destined for export overseas, and the region's transport links were designed above all else to serve this market. The size of the fortunes that could be made in the coal industry in its heyday may have deterred investors from contributing to projects of seemingly less certain potential: certainly south Wales failed to develop any significant manufacturing sector during this period. Ultimately, this was a society built on shifting sands: as the economic historian John Williams has observed, mining is inherently transitory, and 'there is no necessity for an economy based on mining to give rise to a continuing industrial society' (*Was Wales Industrialised?*, 24). In this chapter attention will be devoted to three central aspects of the economic history of the south Wales coal industry in the first half of the twentieth century: struggles to retain existing markets in the face of both serious competition and multiple obstacles; tendencies towards rationalization and concentration of mine size and company ownership; and mechanization and technological change within the industry. There can be no pretence that this will provide a complete anatomy of the industry: it is not yet possible to overcome the many gaps in scholarship and evidence that confront us.

By 1898 the south Wales coalfield was already primarily serving overseas markets, with 56 per cent of its output being exported. Until the Second World War this figure fluctuated between 43 per cent (in 1916, under wartime conditions) and 66 per cent (in 1923, during the French occupation of the Ruhr), and averaged out (1898–1937) at 57 per cent. However, the relative stability of the percentages conceals both an absolute decline in the volume of exports from a peak of 37m tons annually in 1913 to below 20m tons from 1933 onwards, and a continual process of readjustment in response to challenges and obstacles, some internal to the industry, others imposed from without.

In an exporting coalfield, south Wales producers always had to struggle against foreign competitors when developing and securing markets overseas. At its peak, on the eve of the First World War, south Wales coal found its greatest markets in France, Italy, the Low Countries, South America and North Africa. Some of its nineteenth-century markets, in North America, India, and the Middle and Far East, had already shrunk, under pressure from indigenous coal industries in the USA, India and Japan, and those industries' ability to benefit from lower freight costs in proximate markets. More serious competition was to emerge in the 1930s with the rise of the German and Polish coal industries, which also displaced Welsh exports from their domestic markets (as, to some extent, did indigenous coal industries in France and Spain). German coal captured substantial shares of the hitherto Welsh markets in France, the Low Countries, Egypt, Brazil and Argentina, and also challenged Welsh coal in Russia, Greece, Austria, Hungary and French colonial possessions. German coal was also cheaply exported in the form of reparations to Belgium, France and Italy. Poland exported largely to Scandinavia and Italy. Both the German and Polish industries pursued discriminatory pricing policies whereby high domestic prices offset lower prices in the export market. Britain's return to the Gold Standard in 1925 inflated the relative price of south Wales coal in overseas markets, particularly when combined with the devaluation of certain continental currencies shortly afterwards, and in the 1930s France and Spain imposed import limitations or quotas. The inter-war decades were an extremely challenging time for Welsh coal exporters.

Coal producers also had to come to terms with the fact that the demand for coal was being progressively outstripped by the expansion of supplies in the 1920s and 1930s. Oil replaced coal as the preferred fuel for new ships, and the Admiralty switched completely to oil after the First World War. By 1930 its coal order was down to 182,000 tons, an eighth of its pre-war level. More generally, the proportion of coal-driven shipping fell from nearly 90 per cent in 1913 to under 55 per cent in 1932, with major effects on the export of coal for bunker use. Greater efficiencies in the use of coal in electricity generation, in gas, and in the iron and steel industries all combined to reduce demand at home and abroad.

A further problem that faced exporters was the occasional dislocation brought to trade by wars and industrial disputes. Although the First World War resulted in unprecedented demand for south Wales coal from the Admiralty and the domestic market, leading to record profits, this temporarily diverted south Wales coal away from its traditional customers, and total export levels did not recover until 1922. Certain major strikes, by interrupting the production of coal for months at a time, also resulted in the loss of orders, although, again, the dislocation was only temporary. (In 1926, for instance, although exports fell to 11m tons from 26m in 1925, they recovered to reach 28m in 1927.) The traditionally strong market of Italy was affected by sanctions imposed following Mussolini's invasion of

Abyssinia in 1935 (with German coal replacing Welsh coal as a result), and the outbreak of the Spanish Civil War in 1936 severely disrupted Welsh exports there.

All this notwithstanding, it was the relatively high prices demanded for south Wales coal in the export market which most severely damaged its long-term competitiveness. The level of these prices was largely determined not by fluctuations in wages, at least not after the mid-1920s, but by the high costs of production and the relatively low productivity in the south Wales coal industry in comparison with its competitors, many of which mechanized to a far greater extent. The sole success story in terms of exports after the First World War was the anthracite industry. The development of south Wales's anthracite reserves started later than that of steam coal, and anthracite hit its peak production figures in 1934 (over 6m tons), compared with a 1913 peak for the whole of the coalfield. A substantial export market (largely to Europe) was established in the late nineteenth century, and this was followed by the development of the Canadian market in the 1920s. Welsh anthracite producers benefited from strikes in the Pennsylvania coal industry to establish themselves in Canada, and were able to keep freight charges on the transatlantic trade low through the need to find return cargoes for grain shipments from Canada to Britain. A strong domestic market was also built up by the government as an emergency measure during the First World War, and this helped to buttress the anthracite industry against the inter-war depression that so ravaged the neighbouring steam-coal area.

The mixed fortunes (at best) of the south Wales coal industry during the 1920s and 1930s led to various changes in the average size of the unit of production, and in the ownership and economic integration of the industry. In 1910 there were 562 mines in south Wales, with an average work-force per mine of 380 men. By 1929 the total number of mines had fallen to 455, but the average work-force had risen slightly to 409. There was a marked decline in the number of small mines (classed as employing under 250 men) from 369 to 264 between these dates, many closing in the mid- to late 1920s, with a consequent drop in their share of the total work-force from 11 per cent to 8 per cent. Medium-sized mines (250–1,499 men) grew marginally in number from 152 to 157 and from 46 per cent to 55 per cent of the work-force, but large mines (more than 1,500 men) fell in number from forty-one to thirty-four and from 43 per cent to 38 per cent of the work-force. The larger pits often remained open during the late 1920s, but to reduce costs they slashed work-forces and thus fell into the medium-sized category (a pattern that continued into the 1930s and 1940s). By 1947 the extent of even greater rationalization was revealed. Only 222 working mines were taken into public ownership in south Wales, with an average work-force of 482 men. The tendency towards medium-sized mines was marked: 131 mines fell into this category by 1947, employing 80 per cent of all miners. There were only eight large mines, and just eighty-three small mines left, accounting for 13 per cent and 7 per cent of the total work-force respectively.

Such figures conceal wide variations across the coalfield. In the anthracite area small mines were very common owing to the exceptionally fractured geological conditions, with outcrop slants rather than deep-mined pits the normal kind of colliery. Even the largest pits tended to be 'medium-sized', such as Gwaun-cae-Gurwen New Pit which employed 799 men in 1910, or Great Mountain No.1 at Tumble which had a work-force of 1,116 in 1929. Much bigger collieries could be found in the central steam-coal belt, and particularly in the large colliery complexes in the Rhondda Valleys. Thus, in 1910, the Cambrian Colliery at Clydach Vale employed 4,505 men, the Glamorgan Colliery at Llwynypia 3,307, and the Ferndale Collieries had 3,261 men at Ferndale and a further 3,193 at Tylorstown.

Concentrating on the colliery as a unit can often mask more subtle changes in the nature of mining operations. Some collieries contained a number of quite separate sinkings working different seams or districts. Thus at both Ferndale and Tylorstown there were four separate shafts and three different managers. In many cases, particularly in the central areas of the coalfield, the nominal closure of a colliery concealed the fact that its workings were now accessed by a nearby mine. Conversely, a colliery might remain registered as open, but in fact function as little more than a pumping station with a very small work-force for years at a time. For example, the Ynyshir Colliery in the Rhondda Fach, which had employed 1,355 men in 1910, needed only twenty-two to operate pumping by 1929. Quite a number of those pits taken into ownership by the NCB in 1947 were never worked again, and were officially closed a few years later.

Geographically, the worked coalfield exhibited a certain amount of contraction in the inter-war years. Although initially the anthracite coalfield had pushed the boundary west, by the end of the 1930s the balance of employment and production in anthracite had shifted eastwards, to the Neath and Dulais Valleys. By 1938, 44 per cent of all anthracite miners were employed here, compared with 8 per cent in 1901. Many of the more westerly Carmarthenshire collieries were closed and much of the unexploited coal in the Gwendraeth and Amman Valleys was left to the mercy of post-war opencast operations. Shrinkage was also marked along the north crop of the coalfield, where many older collieries were closed as the depression bit. By 1934 not one colliery in the borough of Merthyr Tydfil was left working, and Merthyr itself was at the beginning of 'a melancholy line of semi-derelict communities' along the 'heads of the Valleys' road almost as far as Abergavenny.

The number of colliery companies operating in the south Wales coalfield by the outbreak of the Second World War had contracted with as much rapidity as the number of working mines. The tendency away from fragmented ownership, with a high number of individual companies owning only one or two concerns, towards concentration, whereby a smaller number of companies owned quite possibly half a dozen or more pits, had been noticed before the Great War. The *locus classicus* was the Cambrian Collieries Ltd which, by 1910, controlled not just the Cambrian Collieries at Clydach Vale, but also the Glamorgan Coal Co. Ltd (Llwynypia), the Naval Colliery Co. Ltd (Penygraig) and the Britannic Merthyr Coal Co. Ltd (Gilfach Goch). In addition, the Cambrian's owner, D. A. Thomas, sat on the boards of many other companies, and if these are taken into account then the 'Cambrian Combine' was responsible for the production of around 7.5m tons per annum (13 per cent of the total coalfield output). The Powell Duffryn Steam Coal Co. Ltd was responsible for another 4m tons (7 per cent), and there were four other companies (Ocean Coal and Wilson's Ltd, Guest, Keen and Nettlefolds Ltd, Nixon's Navigation Co. Ltd, and the Ebbw Vale Steel Iron and Coal Co. Ltd) which each produced upwards of 2m tons.

The First World War witnessed further expansion by some of these large concerns. By the time of D. A. Thomas's death in 1918, the Cambrian Combine had acquired the Fernhill Collieries Ltd (Treherbert), the Cynon Colliery Co. Ltd (Pont-rhyd-y-fen), the Duffryn Rhondda Colliery Co. Ltd (Cymmer in the Afan Valley), D. Davis and Sons Ltd (Ferndale, Tylorstown and Pentre), North's Navigation Collieries Ltd (Caerau, Maesteg and Nantyffyllon) and the Gwaun-cae-Gurwen Colliery Co. Ltd. Initially, the Powell Duffryn Company expanded less by means of the purchase of other companies (although it did buy the Rhymney Iron Co. Ltd in 1920 with interests at Rhymney, Bargoed and Pengam) than through sinking large new collieries (such as Ogilvie at Deri near the Rhymney Valley). But with the downturn in the coal trade in the 1920s came opportunities for buying up smaller concerns heading for liquidation. Powell Duffryn bought up the Windsor Steam Coal Co. Ltd (Abertridwr), the Great Western Colliery Co. Ltd (Pontypridd and Llantwit Fardre), the Taff Rhondda Colliery at Nantgarw, and purchased seven pits from the Lewis Merthyr Consolidated Collieries Ltd (Senghennydd, Porth and Ogmore Vale). In 1930 Powell Duffryn purchased the Albion Steam Coal Co. Ltd (Cilfynydd) to give it control of a large swathe of territory in the Rhymney Valley, Pontypridd and Porth areas. In the same year the old Cambrian Combine interests were reorganized as the Welsh Associated Collieries Ltd, controlling no fewer than sixty pits and 32,000 men. This, however, was no longer the economic success it had been two decades earlier, and in 1935 Welsh Associated Collieries Ltd merged with Powell Duffryn to form Powell Duffryn Associated Collieries Ltd, the largest firm in the British coal industry, with over one hundred mines. Powell Duffryn's expansion did not stop there: in 1940 it took over Cilely Collieries Ltd (Tonyrefail), and in 1942 Cory Bros. & Co. Ltd (Treherbert, Ystrad Rhondda, Nantymoel, Ogmore Vale, Resolven). By 1945, Powell Duffryn was responsible for 38 per cent of the total output of the south Wales coal industry. Other major firms that survived the inter-war period were the Ocean and United National Collieries Ltd (responsible for 10 per cent), Partridge, Jones and John Paton Ltd (11 per cent), and the Tredegar Iron and Coal Co. Ltd (6 per cent). Of these, the first had widespread interests reaching from Abergwynfi and Blaengarw across to Risca, with many large collieries in the Rhondda Valleys. The mines of the other two were concentrated in Monmouthshire.

In the anthracite coalfield the tendency towards combination was equally dramatic. Whereas in 1913 there had been over a hundred separate firms operating in this branch of the coal industry, by 1928 the Amalgamated Anthracite Collieries Ltd, run by Sir Alfred Mond, controlled 34 collieries responsible for 80 per cent of anthracite production, and by 1945 it controlled 10 per cent of total coalfield production. Commenting on the extensive holdings of but a handful of huge companies spread across the coalfield, the Communist writer Allen Hutt suggested that 'to journey in South Wales is not to journey from one county or one valley to the next, but to travel from territory to territory of one or other of these combines'.[1]

Almost as significant as the horizontal integration of the south Wales coal industry (between colliery companies) was its vertical integration (with other, related, industries). The interests of coal-owners and the bosses of the giants of the iron, steel and tinplate industries (companies including Guest, Keen and Nettlefolds, Baldwins, and Richard Thomas and Co.) became enmeshed in a complex web of shared directorships and purchases of controlling interests. Sir Evan Williams, president of the Mining Association of Great Britain, was also, variously, director of the Rhymney Iron Company, Oakdale Navigation Collieries Ltd, Cardiff Collieries Ltd, Powell Duffryn, Welsh Associated Collieries, the Tredegar Iron and Coal Company, and Lloyds Bank. Sir Alfred Mond, later Lord Melchett, was director of Amalgamated Anthracite Ltd and of West-minster Bank, and chairman of the chemical company ICI Ltd.

The marked degree of concentration of ownership in south Wales was generally felt to have exacerbated the coalfield's industrial-relations problems. [**DOCUMENT IV**] Any personal connection between an individual coalowner, a single pit, and the mining com-munity that grew up around it was thought to have been severed by the process of combination, although in truth this had often been the case long before 1914. There seemed to be an atmosphere of face-lessness and austerity in industrial relations as the imposition of standardized arrangements across many collieries led to the eradica-tion of traditional customs and concessions at individual pits, and to a widespread sense of frustration, disillusionment and bitterness.

The dramatic changes in the ownership and structure of the south Wales coal industry may be contrasted with the relatively slow pace of mechanization, at least in terms of the introduction of coal-cutting machinery. In 1913, 1 per cent of south Wales output was cut mechanically and this rose to only 26 per cent by 1938 (compared with British averages of 8 and 59 per cent respectively). Given that the introduction of cutters had the potential to double output in a colliery, this might seem a tardy rate of progress. However, it is not necessarily the case that these figures can be read as evidence of poor entrepreneurship or a failure of investment on the part of colliery companies. To begin with, the highly faulted geological nature of the coal strata in south Wales rendered the use of cumbersome cutting equipment inappropriate in many seams. In the anthracite coalfield, in particular, the underground environment was so difficult that mechanization had made very little impact even by 1947. Moreover, such problematic conditions themselves diminished the relative advantage of machinery over muscle-power: south Wales coal was prone, to a much greater degree than that in other British coalfields, to fall of its own accord once undercut. As J. W. F. Rowe wrote in 1923, in south Wales 'the coal breaks away much more easily and the hewers relatively speaking merely have to pull it over'.[2] Finally, in the low-wage economy of the late 1920s and 1930s, the relative cost advantages of the introduction of machinery were considerably lessened, and the unpredictability of the export market often made it economically sensible to employ extra hands as and when required, rather than make the substantial investment of introducing a coal-cutting system.

In any case, technology could be applied in other ways. Pneumatic picks, more flexible than cutting machines, made an impact from the mid-1930s onwards, and by 1944 were responsible for cutting 21 per cent of coalfield output. Electrification of underground workings, coal washing, and ventilation and pumping were all subject to significant technological improvement. Perhaps the most dramatic change was that involved in the introduction of conveyors to carry cut coal away from the coal face. Conveyors were first seen before the Great War, and their use was greatly expanded in the 1920s. By 1931 a fifth of all coal was being conveyed, and this rose to half by 1940, and to just under two-thirds at nationalization.

Mechanization may never have been central to industrial-relations strategies on either side of the bargaining table, but there is no doubt that, where it applied, it did transform working life. Periodically the SWMF voiced serious concerns over the safety of machines, although in the difficult inter-war decades it could not afford to obstruct the introduction of these more economically efficient methods for fear of the mine in question being closed. The rapid advance of coal faces under machine mining was believed to render control of the 'roof' more problematic, as well as to produce greater quantities of gas and dust. Working with machines was noisy, visibility could be poor, and the presence of electric cables presented a further hazard. More significant was the general association of mechanization, certainly in the mind of the miner, with 'speed-up': an intensification of the pace of work with the cutting of corners and a disregard for safety precautions, and a transformation of the collier into 'a mere coal-filling tool'. [**DOCUMENT XI**]

Mechanization also brought with it a transformation of the skills and techniques involved in underground work. New technical knowledge was needed to operate coal-cutters, and although this provided some workers with steady wages and regular employment it deprived others of any livelihood at all. At Bedwas Colliery the introduction of conveyors, pneumatic picks and coal-cutters in the 1920s was the occasion for a wholesale renegotiation (not to the men's advantage) of customs, practices and price-lists. A rigid division of labour was often introduced in parallel with mechanization, and the old single-shift system disappeared under a two- or three-shift system, with cutting, ripping and filling taking place in successive shifts under the close control of colliery deputies. The craft traditions of the collier were discounted, and the control that the hewer in particular had exercised over the pace of his work was diminished. Although the experience of mechanization was highly varied, it heightened tension, frustration and dissatisfaction amongst coal-miners and rendered mining an even less congenial occupation than hitherto.

The received image of the south Wales coal industry in the inter-war period – one of total failure to respond to the demands made of it – is exaggerated. Colliery companies were faced, particularly after 1920, with a series of problems, the most important of which were not of their own making. Given the historically precarious nature of the south Wales coal industry, the fact that in the light of these problems hard choices had to be made should not be surprising. There is little evidence to suggest that coalowners and colliery company directors consistently made, in economic terms, the wrong choices, insofar as it was possible to make the right ones under capitalism. But this is not an apologia for private ownership. The undoubtedly bad reputation of the coalowners by the time the mines were nationalized was not simply – perhaps not at all – the result of a careful assessment of their business record. Rather it was the outcome of a century of industrial-relations hostilities between masters and men, employers and employed, coalowners' association and trade union, with the men who worked in the industry coming to feel that they had been treated merely as economic counters, rather than as human beings worthy of respect. [**DOCUMENT I**]

4.   Trade Unionism

Before the SWMF was founded in 1898, trade unionism had but a slight hold upon those employed in the coal industry in south Wales. The AAM, at its zenith, claimed a membership of 42,161, representing 58 per cent of all those working in the mines. If this figure is accurate then it is both testimony to the success (however temporary) of the AAM and an explanation of the virulent hostility with which it was greeted by the coalowners. Under the Sliding Scale system of wage negotiations, trade unionism was more fragmented and less imperative. Reliable figures are scarce but, at best, an average of only 18 per cent of south Wales miners were unionized between 1892 and 1897, a level of union density that compares poorly with 1895 figures for, for instance, Scotland (25 per cent), Yorkshire (58 per cent), the north-east of England (59 per cent) and even the north Wales coalfield (32 per cent), and was below the British average (39 per cent).

With the foundation of the Fed, however, the coalfield was rapidly unionized. [**DOCUMENT III**] By the end of 1898, the union claimed 60,000 members (47 per cent of the coalfield work-force), and by 1900 this had climbed to 127,894 (87 per cent). Numerically, the union continued to grow up to the First World War, albeit in short bursts interspersed with periods of losses. It numbered 144,580 in 1908, and 153,813 in 1913. But the rapid expansion of the total work-force rendered these figures less impressive as percentages of the whole – 72 per cent in 1908, and only 66 per cent in 1913. In this latter year, south Wales still remained behind many other British coalfields in terms of union density, the British average being 81 per cent.

It is important to remember that throughout most of the period covered by this book those in the mining work-force who stood outside the SWMF were not necessarily outside all trade unions. The South Wales and Monmouthshire Colliery Winding Enginemen's

Association was formed in 1895, before the SWMF, and survived to merge with the South Wales Area of the NUM in 1948. With its motto 'To defend not to defy', it claimed to be able to secure better wages for its members than those obtained by winding enginemen in the SWMF, and in the entire period 1911–47 it had an average annual membership of 800. Of a similar size, and operating at various times within the coal industry, were other minor unions such as the Colliery Examiners' Association, the Master Hauliers' Association, the National Association of Colliery Managers, the Amalgamated Engineering Union, the National Union of General Workers and the National Union of Clerks. The South Wales Colliery Officials' Union was reported to be some 3,000 strong in 1933, and was the largest federation within the General Federation of Firemen's, Examiners' and Deputies' Associations of Great Britain. There was also, briefly, a South Wales Wage Rate Men's Association in Aberdare and Aberaman before the First World War that was a manifestation of tension between hewers on piece-rates and hauliers, surface workers and other men on day-rates. Most significant of all the unions that appealed to specialized grades of worker was the 'Craftsmen's Union', an umbrella term that covered more than one organization and more than one title. Formed as the Monmouthshire and South Wales Colliery Enginemen, Stokers' and Craftsmen's Association in 1889, this had over sixty branches by 1911 and some 9,719 members. Averaging over 7,100 members between 1910 and 1921, it arrived at 'mutual working arrangements' with the SWMF in 1910, established a political fund in 1917 and amalgamated with the SWMF in January 1921. Before the end of that year, however, the South Wales and Monmouthshire Mechanical and Surface Workers' Association (including hitchers, banksmen, surface workers, stokers, enginemen, craftsmen and ostlers) was established, and reportedly attracted around 6,000 members in the early 1920s. By the mid-1930s it was called the South Wales and Monmouthshire Colliery Enginemen, Boilermen and Craftsmen's Association, and had around 1,300 members. It was popularly known as 'D. B. Jones's Union' after its general secretary, and was dissolved in 1938, its members and Jones himself being absorbed into the SWMF.

Accounting for such sectional unions complicates any attempt to assess trade-union density in the south Wales coal industry. Some unions existed for only a few years and had wildly fluctuating memberships; for others detailed membership records are not available. Robin Page Arnot estimated that there were 11,000 men in unions apart from the SWMF in the south Wales coalfield in 1914, and there seems to be no reason to doubt his accuracy. It might be suggested that up to 5 per cent of the total mining work-force could have been organized in various craft or officials' unions at any time during this period, a significant factor when one attempts to measure the success of the SWMF itself in combating both non- and company-unionism. It is true to say that, in theory, the SWMF was, from its inception, committed to the ideal of 'one hundred per cent trade unionism': Object (b) of its Rule 3 was '[t]o secure the entire organisation of all workers employed in and about Collieries in the South Wales and Monmouthshire Coalfield . . .', and in 1920 this was amended to read 'all workers and officials'. Periodically, the Federation pursued vigorous campaigns against the Craftsmen's Union in particular, and argued that its members should be seen as non-unionists and treated as such. This may have been necessary in order to preserve the Fed's position, particularly after 1921, and it is true to say that at least some of those in the Craftsmen's Union who resisted attempts to force them into the SWMF were popularly viewed, abused and remembered as 'scabs'. The same does not seem to have been true of the Winding Enginemen's Association, nor of the organizations of colliery officials and managers. In sum, the bare figures for union density may need adjustment to take into account a further 5 per cent of the work-force in all sectional unions, or just 2 per cent if one discounts the Craftsmen's Union.

This accepted, from 1899 until the 1926 strike, anything between 40 and 91 per cent of the work-force in the coal industry was unionized. This meant that the total number of non-unionists fluctuated dramatically between 12,000 and over 140,000 in any one year, and averaged out at over 64,000 annually. Some of this non-unionism may have been principled: traceable to political objections to the union's policy, to its support of Labour candidates, or to deferential feelings towards individual coalowners. Sir William Thomas Lewis, who had a strong dislike of trade unions, developed the South Wales Miners' Permanent Provident Society from 1881 as part of a deliberate attempt to undermine trade unionism by providing sickness and accident benefits independently. Rhondda Valley Conservative clubs were reported to be encouraging non-unionism in 1923. Other employers and colliery managers attempted to keep local lodges of the SWMF weak by harassing or victimizing union activists, and by breaking up pit-head meetings. But most non-unionism was due either, as Lady Windsor Lodge secretary, John

Morgan, put it, to 'a faulty disbursement of the family income' or to the conditions of rapid labour turnover in this volatile industry. [DOCUMENT II] It was the opinion of the SWMF's financial secretary, Oliver Harris, that 'there are very few non-Unionists on principle employed in the coal industry; 95 per cent of the workmen readily admit that organisation is essential to their welfare'.[1] Much of the evidence bears this statement out. The business of collecting union dues (rather than having them automatically deducted from wage packets at the colliery office, as was to happen from 1942) placed a great burden on both the efficiency of lodge officials, and the budgetary management of individual miners. The SWMF's rules recognized the difficulties: a member could be in arrears for four fortnightly payments before he would lose his benefits, and could go six months in arrears before he would cease to be counted as a member of the Federation, whereupon he would have to pay another entrance fee to rejoin. It is very likely, therefore, both that many men counted as SWMF members were not fully paid-up at all times, and that of the 64,000 non-unionists whom one might expect to find in a given year, many had been Federation members and probably would be again in the near future.

Yet the fluctuating level of non-unionism may also be taken as a barometer of dissatisfaction with the union's performance: its ability to deliver improved wages and conditions, and to protect miners from victimization or the consequences of illness and injury. It is perhaps feasible to read the fall in SWMF membership from 1908 to 1912 (when a total of 30,000 miners drifted away from the organiza-tion) as an indication of disillusionment with the moderate tactics of the union leadership, although the financial strain of the major disputes of 1910–12 may be held equally responsible for the loss of membership. Bouts of unemployment and short-time working also aggravated existing difficulties, and all factors may again have been involved in the startling collapse of union membership from 197,668 (the all-time high) in 1920 to 87,080 in 1922.

Whatever the explanation of such ebbs and flows, the union continually had to be vigilant to ensure a high level of membership in individual pits, lodges and districts. This involved regular 'show-cards' when miners arriving at the pit-head were expected to be able to show a fully paid-up union card, and many stoppages consequent on the unwillingness or inability of some non-unionists to rectify any failings in this respect: [DOCUMENT XII] Between 1898 and 1904 sixty-eight stoppages took place in south Wales on the question of non-unionism, and if individuals refused to succumb to the initial exposure and peer-group pressure, they might find themselves on the receiving end of deputations, demonstrations and even the humiliation of a 'white-shirting'. Up until 1926 such campaigns, if organized competently, were overwhelmingly successful. When a campaign was launched at the Gwaun-cae-Gurwen Colliery in June 1907, out of 130 non-unionists, 126 joined the SWMF and the other four left the district. At the same colliery in April 1922, half the workers were estimated to be non-unionists, but by March 1924 their number had been reduced to only 6 per cent.

There seems to have been considerable variation in union density between lodges, even in the same district, with no discernible pattern according to size of mine. Thus, in the Rhondda No.1 District in 1908, among small mines (under 250 workers) the Gelli House (138 workers) had only 58 per cent of its work-force unionized, but Dinas Isaf (101 workers) managed 89 per cent. Medium-sized mines (250–1,499 workers) ranged in unionization from Lady Lewis (55 per cent) to the Park (92 per cent), and large mines (1,500 workers and above) from Cymmer (56 per cent) to Abergorky (80 per cent).

Much more dramatic variations in unionization both within and across districts can be found after 1926. The total level of unionization (including sectional unions but not including any members of the MIU) ranged between 40 and 89 per cent, the share of the total work-force in the SWMF between 36 and 85 per cent (the two years in question being 1928 and 1939). This compared poorly with, for instance, the Yorkshire Mine Workers' Association, which managed between 59 and an astonishing 98 per cent in the same period, and which averaged 76 per cent. The average annual total of non-unionists (including those in the MIU) remained at 64,000, although fluctuating between 112,000 and 14,000. Of these, it is likely that, at the very most, there were under 8,000 members of the MIU 'on the books' (in 1928), and probably under 2,500 of these were fully paid-up members.

A survey of the level of unionization in individual lodges conducted for 1933 reveals that there were many pits where the MIU had no presence at all, yet where the SWMF was weak or virtually extinct. In this year the average SWMF membership was 44 per cent of the mining work-force. In the Western and Eastern Valleys of Monmouthshire some lodges were well above this average, with 60 per cent unionization or better (North Celynen, Llanhilleth), and others (Markham, Oakdale) had 40–50 per cent of their work-force in the union. Some lodges, however, fell far short of even this moderate target. Less than a quarter of the work-force was in the SWMF at Cwmtillery and Rose Heyworth, and at Wyllie. In the Rhymney Valley, where Powell Duffryn ruled the roost, there was less variation, but only two lodges (Elliots and Groesfaen) achieved figures better than 50 per cent. Further west, the Taff and Cynon Valleys exhibited even poorer results, with Deep Duffryn managing 34 per cent, Penrhiwceiber 16 per cent and Tower a mere 4 per cent. In the Rhondda, once the strongest district by far in the SWMF, some lodges (National, Tydraw) were clinging on at a third of the work-force or better, but most were under 25 per cent and some could scarcely register a presence at all (Llwynypia had fifty-two members out of a work-force of over 1,000, the once-mighty Cambrian 172 out of 2,274). Only when the focus moves west again into the Ogmore, Garw and Llynfi Valleys, and then on into the anthracite coalfield, can one find more encouraging figures. Ffaldau in the Garw was relatively weak at 32 per cent, but the International at Blaengarw managed 59 per cent. In the anthracite area even better percentages were common: Abercrave 67 per cent, Great Mountain 79 per cent, Gwaun-cae-Gurwen 80 per cent. There were exceptions here as well – Morlais 28 per cent, Onllwyn 36 per cent – but Arthur Horner, arriving as agent for the Gwendraeth Valley in that year, had made a wise move from beleaguered Mardy (which had an official membership of just twenty-three out of a workforce of 1,000).

Understandably, it was at those collieries where the MIU had a presence that the SWMF faced its greatest struggle. By 1933 it had already succeeded in driving its rival from some early bases, and Federation membership at the Emlyn (58 per cent) and the Garw Ocean (74 per cent) was more than respectable. At the Raglan and Wern Tarw collieries, the SWMF had 31 per cent and 28 per cent of the work-force respectively, but at MIU strongholds such as the Park and Dare (6 per cent SWMF members), Bedwas (5 per cent), Nine Mile Point (14 per cent) and Taff-Merthyr (no members at all in 1933) it faced an uphill struggle.

The detailed history of the MIU is obscure, and likely to remain so. Its members shared motivations and principles similar in some respects to those of the much larger body of non-unionists. It was encouraged by some colliery companies including the Ocean Coal Company and Instone's, and had links with the Conservative Party, yet some of its most prominent members were more in sympathy with the Liberal Party, or with the Lib-Lab ideal of industrial co-operation. Identifiable motivations amongst its adherents ranged from anti-Communism through a faith in the benefits pertaining to 'non-political' trade unionism, to a more fundamental desire simply to work and earn money at a time when both were in short supply. Many of those prominent in the MIU had been active members of the SWMF, often held representative office within the union, and played significant roles in the wider society. Thus, Will Gooding (president of the MIU in 1928–34) had been a checkweigher at Risca in 1914, vice-chairman of the Nine Mile Point Workmen's Institute and a county councillor. Harry Blount had been on the Oakdale lodge committee and laid the foundation stone at Oakdale Workmen's Institute before losing his job. He spent three years in the MIU before returning to the Federation and, eventually, gaining a place on the lodge committee at Nine Mile Point. Whilst it is true that Powell Duffryn deliberately recruited workers for its mines from as far afield as possible as a deterrent to union solidarity, and although many MIU members who worked in particular pits were bussed in or arrived on the so-called 'ghost train', there were also plenty in the local communities who were far from being 'strangers' or 'foreigners', and who, as Alun Burge has pointed out, 'do not fit easily into the caricature' of a 'scab' ('In search of Harry Blount', 67).

In the end it was the roots that either union could draw on in the communities serving the local pit that were likely to determine the nature of the struggle. The dramatic and imaginative tactical weapon of the 'stay-down' strike, used to great effect by the SWMF in 1935, could not have been successful without much in the way of resources and sympathy above ground. MIU members living locally found themselves on the receiving end of widespread social ostracism, abuse and occasional violence (the pattern was reversed when the MIU was, very occasionally, in the majority). The MIU's best chance of success was the condition, temporarily imposed by certain employers and carried out by the direct deduction of MIU dues, that all workers at particular pits (such as Raglan, Taff-Merthyr and Bedwas) should be members of the union. But against a determined and lengthy campaign by the SWMF, this practice could not be sustained, and ultimately the MIU had neither the leaders, the organization, the funds, the members, the resolve, nor the social centrality to match its rival. In scores of pits across the coalfield the MIU had no presence at all.

The struggle waged between the Federation and the MIU was much more one determined by the former's resolution not to be

displaced and have its representativeness questioned by the coalowners (for in that direction lay, ultimately, disaster and possible
extinction) than characterized by any equal competition between the
two unions for the allegiances of south Wales miners. Even at its
moment of greatest weakness, the SWMF was many times larger
than the MIU. But this struggle was only part of a much wider one to
rebuild the Federation and to drive for 'one hundred per cent. trade
unionism'.

In 1933 this rebuilding involved reorganizing the structure of the
SWMF itself. The Federation was literally that, and had been so
since 1898. It consisted of up to twenty districts, organized mainly
along geographical lines. Within each district there could be dozens
of individual lodges, most based on particular collieries. Each district
elected its own miners' agent, who usually sat on the executive
council along with a number of other district representatives determined by the numerical strength of the district itself, and it sent
delegates to conferences. The annual conference elected the union's
officers. Within each district the agent worked with a district committee of lodge delegates, and within each lodge there would be a
lodge committee, and quite possibly a number of other subcom-
mittees dealing with compensation, recreation, safety and other
issues. Within the SWMF each district had considerable power and
relative autonomy. Some, including many industrial unionists and
syndicalists, felt that this structure inhibited rapid and decisive
action, and they argued for reform along more centralized lines, in
parallel with changes that would reduce the power of the agents.
[**DOCUMENT V**] A rather confused reorganization scheme was
considered by the SWMF in 1912–13 and eventually rejected, but
the problem of lack of co-ordination was exacerbated by the strife
and ravages of the 1920s.

A major difficulty was the disparity in size and strength between
districts. Even before the First World War, some of the larger miners'
lodges, in the Rhondda No.1 District for example, had more
members than the whole of some of the smaller districts (in 1908 the
Cambrian Lodge had 3,183 members, and was larger than the East
Glamorgan, Garw, Ogmore and Gilfach and Saundersfoot districts).
In the 1920s and early 1930s some districts could barely survive as
membership levels tumbled, and it was decided to reform the
structure by concentrating lodges into eight new districts, by
centralizing funds, and by introducing a 'rank-and-file' executive
council which would put decision-making in the SWMF in closer

touch with ordinary miners' experiences, and reduce the power of the district agents.

An additional reorganization involved making an explicit response to the changing nature of coal ownership. The SWMF's reaction to the processes of combination and concentration was to attempt to match the colliery companies pit for pit by organizing its own combine committees, composed of representatives of all concerns held by a single employer. By the late 1920s there were combine committees in the anthracite area, and for the Powell Duffryn, Cory's, Ocean and Cambrian workers, and these could overcome any latent parochialism or 'single-pit' mentality by forming united fronts to co-ordinate negotiations and campaigns against non- and company unionism.

[DOCUMENT IV]

In forming and reforming to meet the changing imperatives of the hostility of employers, the apathy of workers, the rivalry of the MIU and the recasting of capitalism, the SWMF continued to benefit from the position it had established for itself at the centre of mining communities. In 1927 the Federation, no doubt mindful of its precarious position, published a pamphlet outlining the work it felt it had accomplished on behalf of those it represented. One of its first claims was that '[t]here is probably no organization in the world which has such a close relationship to the community it serves as the South Wales Miners' Federation has to the people of the mining areas of South Wales'.[2] This was not only a partisan opinion: according to the 1917 Commissioners of Enquiry into Industrial Unrest, miners' lodges had become 'centres of social and political activity more potent perhaps than any other of the social movements in the community'.[3] If this was true, then trade unionism had supplanted religion as the key provider in civil society, at least in the more homogeneous of the mining valleys. Where the chapels had once delivered social and political leadership in tandem with a spiritual message, the union now brought forward the secular version, and complemented it with a number of material side-benefits as well. Miners' leaders, from the lodge committee man up to the district agent, gave advice and help on a wide range of problems from compensation claims to hire-purchase problems, from rental arrears to the local bus services, and from income tax to where to buy a suit. As Will Paynter wrote, '[i]t was generally believed that a miners' union official was obliged to assist or represent any member of a miner's family in difficulty' ('The "Fed"', 70). Some were better at performing this function than others, and there were those who were stand-offish or partial in their favours. It was in the nature of the job not to be able to satisfy everyone and sometimes trade-union or party politics might inhibit even-handedness on one side of the official–member relationship or appreciation on the other. Equally there were many miners and members of miners' families who did not need or want to seek advice or assistance. Nevertheless, the miners' lodge and the miners' representatives were the focus for many aspects of life in mining communities, well beyond any strictly trade union functions.

To take one example, the Lady Windsor lodge in Ynysybwl was involved in building and controlling the workmen's institute, in running a successful cinema, in providing a hospital and con-valescent-homes fund and an ambulance service, in opening a people's park and a welfare ground, and in securing Labour representation on local governing bodies. One of its pioneers, Abel Morgan, was a founder member of both lodge and the local ILP branch, served on the committee for a quarter of a century, was secretary of the Ocean Combine Committee, a staunch supporter of the Ynysybwl Co-operative Society and the local Labour Party, secretary of the Ynysybwl Recreation Committee, founder member of the Ynysybwl Garden Village Society, secretary of the Workmen's Institute for twenty years, and an urban district councillor. His record was not exceptional, and during the first half of the twentieth century men like Abel Morgan were responsible for redefining their significance in the community, the place of their class in society, and ultimately the very nature of coalfield society itself. It was not a choice between recreation grounds, ambulance teams or the maintenance of rights of way on the one hand, and the class struggle on the other: rather the latter was made concrete, sometimes literally, in the former.

Many miners' leaders spread their involvement 'horizontally' within their own communities, rather than moving onwards and upwards within the Federation or towards Westminster. Of those who did reach high office, often too much has been made of their party-political affiliations. Understandably, men like Arthur Horner stood out because they were card-carrying Communists. But their Com-munism was neither responsible for their success nor irrelevant to it. It was not a choice between electing someone for their ideology or in spite of it. A training in Marxism, or the discipline of the Communist Party, could sharpen the intellect, offer new perspectives and provide spiritual resources when energy flagged or defeat seemed inevitable.

A background in Christian socialism could do the same. **[DOCUMENT VIII]** Essentially all leaders were judged on how effective they were at handling disputes, and at negotiating new price-lists, and here they needed clear-sightedness, a readiness to find common ground, and a keen awareness of when to pick a fight. The best miners' leaders possessed the essentially pragmatic qualities of efficiency, loyalty, tenacity and consistency; and a touch of the firebrand to intimidate the opposition would do no harm at all. Very few leaders, even the most notorious or celebrated, were simply ideologues and rhetoricians.

Some recent writing on the south Wales miners has suggested the existence of a distinct cleavage in the mining work-force between the narrow stratum of 'leaders' and the much wider body of the 'led'. It is clear enough that individual lodges were, by and large, run by small, active minorities. It has been estimated that some 95 per cent of lodge memberships took no active part in trade union affairs to the extent of attending lodge general meetings. This should cause no surprise: much lodge business was relatively mundane, and for every miner willing to devote himself and much of his spare time to union business, there were surely at least twenty with family commitments, leisure pursuits or a desperate need for food and sleep that drew them compellingly away. But this is not to say that union issues did not interest such men: there is considerable evidence to suggest that lodge matters and many other subjects of social and political relevance were discussed at great length on the way to, from and at the mine. And even if only 5 per cent of a lodge's membership attended a general meeting, this could still amount to well over a hundred men present on a monthly basis at some of the larger mines. Higher percentages again attended mass meetings or voted in ballots. Furthermore, there is very little evidence that suggests that the decisions taken by lodge committees or general meetings were seriously out of kilter with the sympathies of the so-called 'rank-and-file' miner, a term that conceals a multitude of different standpoints. The term 'activist' itself covers degrees of involvement, not all of which were necessarily ideological. To sit on a lodge recreation committee or a compensation committee might be proof of nothing more than a genuine desire to improve the lives of one's fellow workers. And it must be remembered that, outside the pit, many 'leaders' and 'activists' shared homes, pubs, clubs, chapels, relatives, perhaps even lovers. Studies of the micro-dynamics of miners' lodges need to delve deeper than the convenient stereotype of the 'activist'/

'rank-and-filer' dichotomy. The SWMF, from its foundation in 1898, managed to establish for itself a place at the centre of coalfield society, and although its survival was, in particular pits and particular communities, sometimes in jeopardy, it never had anything but a direct and umbilical relationship with the people of the mining valleys who created it in their own image.

5.   Politics

Throughout the inter-war decades, the south Wales coalfield provided the Labour Party with its most consistent reservoir of support across Britain as a whole. From the general election of 1918 to the outbreak of the Second World War, there were 118 potential contests at general and by-elections in the fifteen parliamentary constituencies that during that period covered the south Wales coalfield. In these, Labour candidates were victorious in 83, and unopposed in a further 29, making a total success rate of 112 out of 118, or 95 per cent. All six elections in which Labour was unsuccessful came at the general election of 1918. Even at the general election of 1931, disastrous for the Labour Party as a whole, in the coalfield Labour's share of the vote in contested seats rose from 59 per cent (in 1929) to 64 per cent (it went on to 70 per cent in 1935 and 76 per cent in 1945), and the fifteen coalfield MPs represented well over a quarter of the total parliamentary Labour Party.

The very success of the Labour Party in the south Wales coalfield has contributed to a neglect of the area's political history. Images of blanket domination, of miners 'automatically' voting for Labour candidates, have only slowly given way to more subtle understandings of political change and political dynamics. Whereas commentators were once happy to assume that Labour voting was somehow 'natural' in the Valleys, historians are now exploring how this considerable political success was constructed over many years, even decades, and subsequently maintained in the face of an inhospitable economic climate and sporadic challenges from both left and right. What such work reveals is the mosaical nature of political history, whereby each valley, perhaps each township, exhibited a different pattern of allegiance and change. It also demonstrates that changes in the political sphere were not direct reflections of swings in the coal trade or upsurges in industrial militancy, although the vibrations of both were certainly felt. The political arena was a creative as well as a reactive domain, where traditions, institutions, individuals and ideas met and mixed, and in the process generated their own dynamics.

Investigation of the coalfield's political history must begin by analysing the representative structures within which the greater part of such history operated. Between 1885 and 1918 the coalfield was covered by nine parliamentary constituencies returning a total of ten MPs (there being two for the Merthyr Boroughs constituency). In four of these constituencies a majority of the male population of ten years and over were miners (according to the census of 1911): Rhondda (76 per cent), West Monmouthshire (65 per cent), Mid Glamorgan (56 per cent) and East Glamorgan (54 per cent). The remaining six constituencies all included sizeable minorities of miners – Merthyr Boroughs (43 per cent), North Monmouthshire (36 per cent), Gower (26 per cent), South Monmouthshire (22 per cent), South Glamorgan (19 per cent) and East Carmarthenshire (17 per cent) – though some covered large areas of agricultural land as well. In those constituencies where miners predominated amongst the work-force, their numerical weight amongst the parliamentary electorate was likely to be somewhat less, for a number of reasons. First, it is likely that a slightly higher than average proportion of all those working in the industry were below the franchisable age of twenty-one. Second, although the franchise did not operate with a very heavy anti-working-class bias, it was effectively biased against recording younger men and lodgers, whilst those with high levels of geographical mobility (which could include miners moving from one district to the next in search of work) could easily fall foul of the residence requirement which demanded a year's presence in a constituency. Finally, those who had recourse to the poor law were automatically disfranchised, and this regulation had a severe impact in mining constituencies in the wake of serious industrial disputes.

[DOCUMENT VI]

Structural obstacles such as these played some part in restricting Labour's parliamentary advance before the First World War. Divisions and mutual antipathies within the labour movement between individuals, trade unions, and settlements also had an effect. Thus, at the Gower election in 1900 the steel smelters' leader, John Hodge, found his candidature opposed by the local miners and their leader, John Williams (who went on to win the seat in 1906). The very moderate leadership of the SWMF was disinclined to threaten the stability of the 'progressive alliance' at the general election of

January 1910 by running candidates in all the seats it had designated
as 'miners' seats', and withdrew candidates in three seats where they
would have clashed with Liberal rivals. Even at the East Carmarthenshire by-election of 1912, J. H. Williams found that very little support
came his way from the SWMF.

The Liberals must also be credited with some success in
maintaining their representation in the face of growing pressure from
Labour, at least until the First World War. They were fortunate in that
they did not have to face serious challenges from the Conservative
Party (which managed to hold just one of the seats already
mentioned, South Glamorgan from 1900 to 1906) and could concentrate on holding the line against Labour, but their success must
be ascribed less to their organizational efficiency and their candidates' charisma and more to the image of social harmony and national
prosperity that they could graft on to their traditional objectives of
disestablishment and land reform. Ultimately such policies did not
suffice, and the benevolent image of Welsh Liberalism collapsed
amidst the horrors of the First World War and the bitterness of its
aftermath.

The picture of slow progress obtained from a study of Labour bids
for parliamentary success must be qualified somewhat by evidence
indicating wider support for the Labour Party amongst miners in
particular. Clear support for the principle of MFGB affiliation to the
Labour Party was first demonstrated by the ballot of 1906, which
witnessed a 41,843–31,527 vote (representing a turnout of 61 per
cent) in favour in south Wales, although it was countermanded by a
small majority against the proposal across Britain as a whole. At the
1908 ballot SWMF members were clearer still in their support,
voting 74,675–44,616 (a turnout of 82 per cent), and this time were
on the winning side. Even those who voted against affiliation – the
Lib-Labs – have to be credited with making a significant contribution
to the development of the independent political structures of the
labour movement, for they had sustained miners' candidates and
representatives for some years in complete separation from any local
Liberal Association, even if ostensibly they shared the same ideals.

The relative popularity of doctrines of syndicalism and industrial
unionism in the south Wales coalfield before 1914 made little
difference to the political advance of the labour movement. Although
there were a few within the circles of the Unofficial Reform
Committee who denied the necessity of any political activity, most
recognized its utility and many were practising councillors or

activists in the ILP, Trades and Labour Councils or in a local Labour Party structure. Political action remained subordinate to the need to reform the SWMF and the wider trade union movement, and to fight battles in the industrial arena, but it was rarely disavowed altogether. **[DOCUMENT V]**

The First World War offered Labour representatives a chance to 'prove' themselves in administering the local state: many served on committees dealing with pensions, servicemen's dependants, food control and rents and rates, others took up positions on military tribunals and participated in recruiting drives. At a British level, Labour attempted to appeal to the widest possible constituency with a broad church of progressive ideas, and a focus on pragmatic, realizable goals that could be achieved, it was believed, through the liberal state. The attainability of power, via Labour, reinforced by the electoral successes of the 1920s, proved a powerful attraction to many socialists.

The electoral reforms of 1918 removed most of the afore-mentioned structural obstacles to working-class enfranchisement. All males aged twenty-one and over gained the vote, along with women over thirty (over twenty-one from 1928). The poor-law disqualification was ended, and the registration system simplified. In tandem with changes in electoral law came a redistribution of constituencies which in effect created a bloc of fifteen single-member coalfield seats: Aberavon, Aberdare, Abertillery, Bedwellty, Caerphilly, Ebbw Vale, Gower, Llanelli, Merthyr Tydfil, Neath, Ogmore, Pontypool, Pontypridd, Rhondda East and Rhondda West. In ten of these seats miners were in an absolute majority of the male population aged twelve and over (according to the census of 1921), reaching up to 74 per cent in the Rhondda Valleys. In the remaining five they again constituted a sizeable minority, alongside other industrial workers: 27 per cent in Aberavon, 28 per cent in Llanelli, 33 per cent in Gower, 45 per cent in Neath and 48 per cent in Pontypool. Without exception, from the 1922 general election onwards, all fifteen constituencies were held by the Labour Party. In two other constituencies (Carmarthen, and Brecon and Radnor) miners constituted over one-fifth of the male population, but their votes tended to be swamped by those of their preponderantly rural co-constituents, as the share of the work-force in agriculture was higher than that in mining.

Below the level of parliamentary representation were the tiers of local government. These were the county councils (Glamorgan,

Monmouthshire and Carmarthenshire), the county borough of Merthyr, the borough councils (Llanelli, Neath, Port Talbot), the many urban district and rural district councils, and, up to 1930, the poor law Boards of Guardians. Labour had had a presence on some local councils before 1914, but the local elections of 1919 propelled it into power at the expense of the Liberals and Independents who had hitherto been dominant. Both Glamorgan and Monmouthshire County Councils fell to Labour, along with urban district councils including Bedwellty, Ebbw Vale, Maesteg, Nantyglo and Blaina, Ogmore and Garw, Rhondda, and Tredegar. Although control was lost on some of these bodies in 1922 (both county councils, for instance), by the end of the 1920s Labour was indisputably the dominant party in local government in the coalfield, with no fewer than twenty authorities under its sway. Such control was intensified in the 1930s so that by the eve of the Second World War well over thirty authorities were run by Labour councillors.

The record of Labour in local government defies easy assessment, but it is fair to say that, well into the 1920s, Labour councillors took office often on radical platforms which displayed considerable awareness of the potential of local government services for improving the lives of their communities. Thus, in Tredegar in 1919 the party suggested introducing electric lighting, improving local transport facilities and supplies of gas and water, establishing a stipendiary magistracy and addressing the problem of subsidence. In Pontypridd in 1920 Labour proclaimed that it would municipalize the milk supply, improve local sanitation, combat river pollution, develop public parks and build new houses. In Rhondda, Labour also attempted to implement a major house-building scheme. Unfortunately for many ruling Labour groups, local government finances were already under considerable strain and central government support was insufficient to allow many of these objectives to be realized. Instead, such groups often found themselves in the uncomfortable position of having to impose wage restraint on municipal employees (including teachers) in order to keep rate rises down to politically acceptable levels.

Some ruling Labour groups experienced severe internal tensions over such matters, exacerbated by the crisis of local government finance that accompanied the rising unemployment and strike activity of the mid-1920s. In some local authorities one can identify divisions between what may be labelled 'pragmatist' and 'rejectionist' groupings within the Labour Party. The 'pragmatic' strategy was to work the system to maximum advantage, but to recognize the limits of power, particularly the financial limits, and to be aware both of the coercive mechanisms open to a hostile central government, and of the responsibilities that the labour movement had to its constituents. The 'rejectionist' strategy, in contrast, was far less tolerant of constraints on policy, and in rhetoric at least was prepared to carry the struggle to the central government. Thus, over the poor law, both Communist Arthur Horner in Rhondda and Labour socialist Aneurin Bevan in Tredegar fought for higher scales of outdoor relief for the poor, and for the non-repayment of money loaned to miners by the Boards of Guardians during the lockout of 1921. Yet in Tredegar, Bevan's mentor Walter Conway argued that the Guardians, acting in isolation, had no chance of changing government policy. Other 'pragmatists' such as Noah Tromans of Mountain Ash and later Ferndale, who was the chairman of the Pontypridd Board of Guardians by the early 1920s, believed that the 'rejectionist' strategy would result not in overturning the system but in bankruptcy and in handing over local government institutions which the Labour Party had struggled long and hard to win to the draconian agents of central government. Generally Labour groups decided that it was better to continue to administer even relatively harsh regulations, with as much sympathy as possible, than to abdicate control to 'faceless bureaucrats' with no commitment to the area and its people. During the 1930s Labour local authorities, despite operating within strict financial constraints, were able to alleviate some of the worst features of the Depression through resourceful policy initiatives, including the establishment of maternity and child welfare clinics and an extensive road-building scheme carried out by Glamorgan County Council. Overall, Labour groups can be judged to have put up a competent performance in very difficult circumstances. [**DOCUMENT XIII**]

Nevertheless, a serious criticism levelled at the record of the Labour Party in local government in the Valleys was that its domination fostered a 'one-party state' within which nepotism and corruption could flourish. Investigation of such murky affairs is difficult. There is little doubt that some nepotism (typically finding jobs for relatives) and corruption (including taking bribes in order to vote for particular applicants for council posts) were present, and that they involved only a minority of councillors. Most had no association with such matters, and some made it their business to expose wayward comrades, even if this led to the political and electoral embarrassment of the Labour Party. There is further evidence that such practices were known under Liberal-controlled councils, and that Communists were not immune to such temptations. More significant may be the fact that many of those who were believed to be involved in such practices were elected and re-elected by their constituents many times over many years, suggesting at least an element of public tolerance.

As with the SWMF, so the Labour Party had important roots in the structures of the community. Party representatives and activists were social as well as political animals, serving in a variety of capacities in trade unions, religious organizations, and in voluntary associations covering everything from pigeon-fancying to rugby union, and from radio-hamming to eisteddfodau. They encompassed men and women enmeshed in their communities who had succeeded, often after a long struggle, in generating a new sense of community leadership that replaced the more deferential and personality-based patterns of the Liberal era. The cultural dimension of political organization and activity must be appreciated if the often opaque relationships between working-class parties and their communities are not to be misconstrued. [**DOCUMENT IX**]

Generally Labour identified with the wider coalfield society, rather than representing any 'alternative' path. In some areas Labour activists made attempts to provide an 'all-embracing' party culture that would reinforce group loyalties and attract members, and to this end staged Labour pageants, May Day demonstrations, and carnivals, and ran Labour choirs, orchestras, bands, amateur dramatic societies, youth clubs and sports teams. But such efforts were far from widespread, and usually petered out after a few years, occasionally being revived in the mid-1930s in response to the Communist challenge. Whether it was football or cinema, the public house or the allotment, working-class culture was much more protean and extensive than anything that could be provided by a political party, and Labour activists' links with the community were material recognition of this fact. Similarly, Labour did not make a dramatic break with religion: many Labour public representatives were practising Christians, chapel deacons, some even lay preachers. Gradually, as Labour's domination of coalfield politics acquired a permanent character, so ministers of religion warmed to the new community leaders. [**DOCUMENT XIV**]

Labour's ability to provide political leadership was reinforced by the establishment of a much stronger organizational structure in the party after the adoption of a new constitution in 1918. By 1924 every constituency had its own Labour Party, and although the support of the trade unions, particularly the SWMF, remained critical, individual membership of constituency Labour parties (CLP) tended to replace the older ILP. By the 1930s, the average member-ship of a coalfield CLP was 760, with the largest parties (sometimes with over 1,000 members) found in those areas where the SWMF was not totally dominant (Caerphilly, Aberavon, Pontypool, Neath and Pontypridd). Other CLPs were, however, very small, averaging under 500 members (Aberdare, Abertillery, Merthyr Tydfil, Ebbw Vale). Such low levels of membership are in part explicable by the overwhelming success that Labour enjoyed: maintaining an efficient electioneering structure and 'working' the constituency were not usually necessary for it to win votes. Following its clean sweep of the parliamentary chessboard in the coalfield in 1922, Labour was subject to only fitful challenges from the political right during the remainder of the 1920s and 1930s. Its most marginal seat was Pontypool, held in 1923 with a majority of only 256, but here in 1924 the Liberals gave way to a Conservative candidate, and the majority was increased to over 1,500 votes. Ramsay MacDonald was sufficiently uncomfortable with the size of his majority in Aberavon (2,100 votes in 1924) to seek a seat elsewhere, and Labour also needed to remain vigilant in Llanelli, but when three-cornered contests became the norm at the 1929 election Labour won all its seats with considerable ease (the lowest majority, in Pontypool, was still over 5,000).

Neither the Liberal nor Conservative Party was able to respond effectively to Labour's success. The organization of both these parties was frequently moribund or non-existent, and unable to cope with the new demands of a mass electorate. Their parliamentary cam-paigning was too often characterized by the 'getting up' of candid-ates, often imported from outside the constituency, at short notice. Some of the most effective displays came when the two parties combined to back a single 'Coalition' or 'Anti-Labour' candidate, but rarely was such an arrangement sustained with the same candidate in place for more than one election, and dismay amongst supporters and confusion amongst the wider electorate were invariably the outcome. The Liberal Party did make a sustained effort in the mid-to late 1920s to revitalize its policies, and its 'Coal and Power' programme attracted interest from a number of miners' leaders in the wake of the 1926 débâcle, such as from Jack Jones (who subsequently joined the Liberal Party) and James Griffiths (who did not), but the party's disastrous showing at the 1929 election effectively killed off any chances of a revival. Lloyd George, it seemed, had lost the trust of the miners permanently following his handling of the Sankey Report in 1919. As for the Conservatives, G. H. Armbruster summed things up neatly: 'The Conservatives are locally despised, the party is associated with everything that is resented and hated, it is a polar symbol representing all that brings misfortune and insecurity.'[1] Even the large and popular Conservative clubs that were sprinkled up and down the Valleys concealed quite different allegiances. In the Sirhowy Valley in the 1930s, the Cwm-felinfach club was dominated by miners loyal to the SWMF and intent on ousting the MIU from the nearby Nine Mile Point colliery, whilst in the Rhondda Fach the Ferndale Conservative club was actually populated by members of the Communist Party. Other clubs were supported as much by 'drinking' as by 'thinking' members.

Nor was south Wales hospitable territory for 'fringe' movements. Oswald Mosley's New Party ran two candidates at the 1931 election, and whilst William Lowell polled only 466 votes in Pontypridd, Sellick Davies managed a remarkable 10,834 votes in Merthyr Tydfil, albeit supported in a two-horse race by Conservatives and Liberals. But any hopes that Mosley may have had of building on this vote evaporated when his New Party was replaced by the British Union of Fascists (BUF). In its heyday in 1934, the BUF claimed to have branches in Merthyr, Rhondda and Bargoed, but no records survive to indicate how strong or persistent these were. There were later intimations of support in the Ebbw Vale and Pontypool areas, and BUF activist Arthur Eyles, a former member of the Communist Party, did run (without success) in local elections in 1937 and 1938, but the overwhelming response of the coalfield to Fascism was one of sustained hostility and vigorous opposition, with public meetings at Neath in 1934, and at Tonypandy and Pontypridd in 1936 being disrupted. As for Plaid Cymru, it fielded candidates in three coalfield constituencies (Neath, Ogmore and Rhondda East) at the 1945 election, coming last in each and averaging 6 per cent of the vote. The Neath result put into perspective a much better showing in a by-election there in May 1945, when Plaid had polled 16 per cent in the context of an electoral truce agreed by the major parties. Overall, Plaid Cymru's association with a Welsh-speaking élite which seemed to exhibit little or no sense of the problems of working people, and which was prepared to countenance the deindustrialization of the south Wales valleys, was hardly likely to win it much support in an area where deindustrialization needed no encouragement. By the mid-1930s the closest challengers to Labour were neither the Liberals nor Conservatives on the right but the Communists on their left. In 1935 the Communist leader Harry Pollitt, standing in Rhondda East and building on the foundations of three candidatures by Arthur Horner in 1929, 1931 and 1933, picked up 38 per cent of the vote, and subsequently came within a thousand votes of the Labour MP, W. H. Mainwaring, in 1945. However, in every other coalfield constituency Labour continued to measure its majority by the bucketful.

There were thirty-eight Communist Party branches in south Wales by 1927, with a membership of 2,300. But Communism remained very much a minority identification, in terms of votes and members. Communist Party support was limited by perceptions of its atheism and hostility to democracy. Neither picture was fully accurate. The Communist Party tended to be the most active of all political groups in the coalfield, holding lively meetings, and securing a reputation for effective work on local government bodies. Communist councillors tended to exhibit an embeddedness in the community very similar to that of their Labour rivals. Most Communists were or had been active in the SWMF, some were chapel deacons, and ideological commitment of whatever flavour counted for nothing if it was not expressed in bonds of human attachment between politicians and people. Communist activists were also predominantly drawn from the same mining work-force as Labour activists, although Communists were less likely to be found amidst the ranks of municipal employees, transport workers, white-collar workers, small business-men and professionals.

The Communist Party was more successful than Labour in providing a distinctive, separate culture. Most of its members by the 1930s were unemployed and involved in the National Unemployed Workers' Movement. Communist activists were joined in a political community of shared values and perspectives, and participated in distinct social patterns that could include Communist soccer teams, newspapers, parades and funerals. The Communists were, to para-phrase Gwyn A. Williams, a contagious minority which charged the south Wales labour movement with power, internationalism, and colour.[2] Nevertheless, that they had political space within which to operate was largely a function of Labour's overwhelming success in routing Liberal and other opposition and in providing a secure environment for the contemplation of more extravagant alternatives to parliamentary socialism. The development of 'revolutionary' strategies such as syndicalism and Communism took place within the context of a more general Labour hegemony, and all organizations on the left inhabited a common cultural terrain.

Often set apart from orthodox party politics was the political development of the 'women's movement'. The campaign for the vote had a minor presence in the coalfield before 1914. There were branches of the National Union of Women's Suffrage Societies at Bargoed, Pontypool, and in Rhondda, and there was also some interest in the Women's Social and Political Union, although the absence of women from the ranks of the paid employed, and the domination of local political structures by the miners, left few opportunities for the politicization, let alone activism, of women as a group. [DOCUMENT XV] The characteristic form of involvement came through the Co-operative Women's Guild, which had extensive coverage in south Wales in the inter-war period, and through the women's sections of the Labour Party. By the 1930s women made up around 45 per cent of Labour Party individual membership in the coalfield, with particularly high rates being found in Abertillery (59 per cent) and Rhondda (62 per cent), although such numerical domination was not reflected in the numbers of women on the party's executive councils, or as local government representatives. Some of these women were fully-fledged politicians in their own right: in Pontycymmer in the Garw Valley, Sarah Jones had been a suffrage campaigner and a member of the ILP before involving herself in the women's section. Women such as Elizabeth Andrews, the Labour Party's women's organizer in Wales from 1919, campaigned on issues relevant to miners' wives, such as housing and pithead baths, and women were also to the fore in demanding maternity and child welfare clinics. [DOCUMENT XVI] Others operated very much within a traditional 'tea-making' and fund-raising sphere, and there was relatively little 'equal-rights feminism' to be found in the coalfield during this period. Even Mrs Winifred Griffiths, the wife of the later president of the SWMF, writing about 'Co-operative housekeeping' in 1925, saw social improvements as helping to make 'joyous, healthy and happy women – true comrades to their menfolk, and willing mothers of happy children!'[3]

The other political movement which does not fit neatly inside party-political boundaries was that concerned with a series of social issues, most of which could be found all over Wales, but many of which had specific relevance to the south Wales coalfield. By the end of the first decade of the twentieth century, a number of youngish, educated men in their thirties and early forties, and occasionally women, were convinced of the need to intervene in the public life of Wales. They included Daniel Lleufer Thomas, Edgar Chappell, Thomas Jones and Miss E. P. Hughes, and politically they were a mixed bag: some Liberals, some Labour supporters or Fabians, others explicit socialists, one or two Conservatives. Generally they shared in the progressivism and 'new liberalism' of the time, and felt that an alternative was needed to what seemed to them to be an existing choice between the evils of unrestrained capitalism and the increasingly worrying militancy of the organized labour movement. Their guiding principle was to find a middle way, to reconcile capital and labour, employer and employee, and to work for a common citizenship and for general reformism. They identified social evils that demanded remedies: tuberculosis, the absence of pit-head baths for miners, poor housing, unemployment, and the destruction of what they understood to be Welsh culture. To combat these perceived blights, they formed associations and published magazines (such as the *Welsh Outlook*), and increasingly took up important posts in the structure of government and administration in Wales. They were behind the university settlement movement, the Workers' Educational Association, the adult education college, Coleg Harlech, the Welsh Housing and Development Association, the anti-tuberculosis campaign, and the social-service and voluntarist movements of the 1930s. Many of these movements involved Labour and miners' leaders as well: notably Vernon Hartshorn, William Jenkins and James Winstone. Richard Lewis has suggested that they 'formed a bridge between the old Liberal radicalism and the new socialist labourism', and through consensus and persuasion contributed much to the developing political culture of Wales ('The Welsh radical tradition', 340). Their analyses lent intellectual weight to the growing body of calls for greater state intervention in economic and social affairs, ultimately realized after the Second World War.

The politics of the south Wales coalfield were manifestly vibrant and controversial throughout this period. Yet the impact on any wider political stage was limited. Most home-grown MPs, Liberal or Labour, had only moderately successful political careers, the exceptions being Reginald McKenna, D. A. Thomas, Vernon Hartshorn, James Griffiths and Aneurin Bevan. Relatively few found their way into governments, even as junior ministers. This was in part owing to the fact that the traditional way to the Commons for aspirant

Labourites was a lengthy rise through the structures of the SWMF (over four-fifths of coalfield MPs had been miners), combined with some service on a local government body, with a parliamentary candidacy arriving as much as a reward for time served as a recognition of political aptitude. Yet, whatever its limitations outside the coalfield, Labour domination was the reflection of a consistent popular will, and became an integral element of the culture of the mining valleys. [**DOCUMENT XVII**] As Roger Fagge has noted, 'in an increasingly national political framework, the web of identities – Welsh, English, British, radical, socialist, working-class, miner – which were the substance of these communities became redefined, and reshuffled around the appeal of the pragmatic Labour Party' (*Power, Culture and Conflict*, 254).

6. Society

Writings about the history of the south Wales coalfield, whether by governments, journalists, politicians or academics, have often generated a one-dimensional image in which the coal industry and the workers within it have become synonymous with the coalfield as a whole. Economically and politically such an impression is accurate enough, being little more than a direct reflection of the preponderance of both coal and miners in the region's economic and political structures. However, any attempt to construct a rounded understanding of coalfield society cannot ignore the presence of divisions, complications and contradictions which belie the received image of a homogeneous, organic whole.

This chapter considers three such divisions, or lines of social fracture: those of gender, ethnicity (encompassing national, linguistic and religious identities), and poverty and its twin, unemployment. These themes have been chosen because they were fundamental elements in how individuals defined themselves and were defined by others: as a man or woman, as a member of a particular ethnic group, as unemployed or poor. It does not offer a complete picture of social life in the south Wales coalfield: matters such as childhood, diet, dress, health, housing and leisure, all of which might be determined by gender, ethnicity or poverty, are mentioned in passing rather than discussed. Nevertheless, since societies may best be understood by what they exclude, by what lies beyond their boundaries, the following pages offer an analytical approach which seeks to raise significant questions concerning the received image of a homogeneous coalfield society.

The most significant long-term omission in most social histories of the south Wales coalfield is a rounded appraisal of gender relations. Much work has still to be done before a full understanding can be reached of how discourses of masculinity and femininity were articulated and sustained, and how women in particular were confined within a restricted 'private sphere' whilst their menfolk achieved and celebrated a reputation for a distinctly radical public culture. What is clear, however, is that such a separation of spheres was pointedly expressed in the relative absence of paid work for women across the coalfield.

The decennial population censuses are recognized as inefficient tools for measuring the absolute level at which women engaged in paid employment, but they offer the most consistent standard by which the relative participation of women in the economy may be gauged. Even assuming an element of under-recording of women's work, there is little reason to doubt that, in the south Wales coalfield, women had a marginal place in the work-force. The prohibition of female labour underground and the absence of any significant manufacturing sector in the Welsh economy meant that women seeking work had a very restricted range of occupations from which to choose. Linked to this economic reality was a domestic ideology, conventional enough across British society at the time, which stressed that a woman's place was very much in the home, attending to the needs of her husband. This could be reinforced by informal or formal 'marriage bars' which required women to leave work upon marriage, and by a general sentiment that, when there were men out of work, it was wrong for women to be in employment, unless they were the sole remaining breadwinner in a household. A study of the census taken in 1921, at the height of the coal industry's predominance in the labour force in south Wales, reveals the consequences of both these forces, economic and ideological.

In 1921, taking the counties of Glamorgan and Monmouthshire together, only 19 per cent of the female population over twelve were recorded as occupied, the remaining 81 per cent being 'unoccupied or retired' (for males the comparable figures were 89 per cent occupied and 11 per cent unoccupied or retired). The British average at this time for female 'economic activity' was 33 per cent, indicating that women in the coalfield counties had considerably fewer chances of finding paid employment than did many elsewhere in the country. Examination of the figures for the mining valleys themselves reveal even lower rates of economic activity for women: Pontypool (23 per cent) and Neath Borough (22 per cent) were the only local authority areas to reveal above-average levels for the two counties, with all others falling below. Levels of 13 per cent (Abercarn, Blaenavon,

Ebbw Vale, Gelligaer, Mountain Ash, Rhondda and Risca) were common, and the lowest rates (11 per cent) were found in Glyncorrwg, Mynyddislwyn, and Nantyglo and Blaina. In Carmarthenshire higher (if still below the national average) levels of women were in work (23 per cent), though much of this was due to agricultural employment.

The significance of these figures becomes clearer still once the age and marital structure of the female work-force is assessed. In the Rhondda Urban District for example, only 13 per cent of women between the ages of twenty and forty-four, and 6 per cent of those between forty-five and sixty-four, were in work, in contrast to 33 per cent of those between sixteen and nineteen. Of married women in the same area, only 2 per cent of those aged forty-four and under, and 3 per cent of those who were forty-five or over were economically active. In the two counties together, single women accounted for 83 per cent of the work-force, widowed and divorced women 8 per cent and married women only 9 per cent. Well over half of the female work-force was under twenty-four years of age.

As might be expected, the women who comprised 17 per cent of the total work-force (male and female) in Glamorgan and Monmouthshire were concentrated in particular sectors of the economy, with relatively little variation across the coalfield: 40 per cent in 'personal service' (mainly as domestic servants but also including charwomen, lodging-house and inn keepers, barmaids, and laundry workers), 18 per cent in commercial and financial occupations (mostly shop assistants, some shop proprietors), 11 per cent in professional occupations (teaching and nursing), 10 per cent in 'textile goods and dress' (dress and blouse makers, tailoresses, embroiderers and milliners) and 7 per cent in clerical and typing jobs. Only in the western parts of Glamorgan and eastern Carmarthenshire was an industrial occupation, in the shape of the tinplate trade, open to women in any number. In the early 1920s over 3,000 overwhelmingly unmarried women were employed in this industry, representing around 15 per cent of the total work-force, and in the Swansea, Neath and Afan Valleys this sector of the economy accounted for between 10 and 19 per cent of women workers. In Llanelly Borough there were 700 such workers in 1921, representing 21 per cent of the female labour-force. Within the industry, men's work and women's work remained clearly demarcated, with women taking the least skilled and worst-paid jobs. There was also some female employment in the metal trades in the

Eastern Valley of Monmouthshire, where a number of young women worked at the Pontnewydd Tin Stamping Works, making tins for tobacco and sweets.

When assessing the low rates of economic activity for women in the south Wales coalfield, it is necessary to bear in mind that the official census failed to record remunerative work undertaken by women on a casual, temporary, seasonal or informal basis. This could include charring for neighbours, taking in other people's washing and sewing, even taking in lodgers, or making beer, lemonade, cakes, sweets, faggots or brawn for sale. For some married women and widows this was the only work that was open to them. **[DOCUMENT XVIII]** Another aspect of female economic experience that is not revealed by a study of the census for Glamorgan and Monmouthshire is that of young women moving away to work as domestic servants in the west, Midlands, south and south-east of England. Often the expectation here was that they would work away for a few years, returning home to settle down and marry, though as the Depression of the late 1920s and 1930s bit deeper, many remained in England on a permanent basis. Finally, during the Second World War three Royal Ordnance Factories were opened in south Wales (at Hirwaun, Glascoed and Bridgend), and smaller factories were also established at Newport and Cardiff, at which many thousands of women were employed. Bridgend had a workforce of over 30,000 at its peak, of which 70 per cent were female, and married women formed a significant part of the munitions workforce by the end of the war. However, many returned to a life of domesticity with the onset of peace, and the 1951 census recorded only a quarter of Glamorgan and Monmouthshire women in work, compared with a British average of a third.

Women's work was, then, highly segregated from that of men, and generally located in relatively low-waged and low-status sectors of the economy. **[DOCUMENT XIX]** Work tended to be something that women did in their teens and early twenties, and which ended with their marriage. Marriage itself came early in the coalfield: 44 per cent of Monmouthshire women under twenty-five were recorded as married by the 1921 census, compared with an England and Wales average of 29 per cent. This was, in material terms, a function of three features of coalfield society: the absence of long-term career (or even simply working) structures for women that not only rendered early marriage more likely but also often forced widows to seek new husbands out of economic necessity; second, the numerical predominance of men over women in the mining valleys; and, finally, the relatively high wages that could be earned at a young age by coal-hewers and which facilitated the establishment of separate households, traditionally a prerequisite for marriage, albeit one that was increasingly compromised in the years of economic depression.

Early marriage may also have been a more direct function of pre-marital pregnancy. Evidence as to the extent of premarital sexual activity in the coalfield is sparse and has to be treated with great caution, but there is good reason to believe that it was engaged in by many courting couples, not all of them intending to go on to marry. Widespread ignorance, allied to the expense and unreliability of commercially available contraceptives, meant that many liaisons ended either in the shame of an extra-marital pregnancy (which seems to have been generally frowned upon) or in a hastily arranged wedding (which seems to have been accepted, and the circumstances of which were quickly forgotten). Reliable information on the prevalence of abortion and infanticide is extremely limited, but most communities included women who could be 'sent for' if the former were desired, and newspapers carried many advertisements for aborti-facients such as lead pills. Only slowly, and against considerable hostility from organized religion and from many male politicians, was advice on birth control officially made available, usually to married women only, in maternity and child welfare clinics; most women had to fall back on the not-always-reliable advice of friends and relatives.

Upon marriage, women traded any degree of wage-earning capacity and economic and personal independence they may have enjoyed for economic dependence upon their husbands and a life of hard and unwaged domestic labour. It was said in 1921, when miners were working a seven-hour day, that their wives worked for seventeen hours, performing tasks that were vital to the maintenance of their households and to their husbands' effective functioning as employees. The nature of the mining industry itself imposed strains upon women: there was always the possibility that their loved ones would be killed or injured at work, and there was the certainty that miners would return home after their day's work dirty and often wet. With the first pit-head baths not opening until 1914, and with a majority of miners still without access to such facilities at national-ization, the miner's wife would have to boil large pans of water in order for a tin bath to be taken in front of the fire. [**DOCUMENT XVI**] Bathrooms equipped with hot water were rare – only 2 per cent of working-class homes in the Rhondda in 1920 had baths – whilst if a woman had sons or lodgers as well as her husband to cater for, her work in cleaning and drying their clothes as they came off shift would be increased in proportion. Such difficulties were exacerbated if the males of the household worked on different shifts: a wife might then be engaged in a near-constant cycle of preparing baths and food. Add child-care and the problems of running a household in often cramped and overcrowded conditions and it is easy to understand why few married women could have had either the energy or the time for even part-time paid work, given the full-time labour that was required and expected of them at home.

That most women triumphed over such inhospitable conditions and onerous demands, carrying their partners and children through decades of often adverse circumstances, is testament to their determination, and to the strength of the domestic ideology that conditioned them to accept their lot as, if not 'natural', then at least inescapable. High standards of cleanliness and a strict pattern were imposed on housework, with particular days set aside for certain tasks such as washing, ironing, baking and cleaning. Washing by hand, scrubbing floors, steps and flagstones, cooking over a coal stove, battling against the persistent incursions of coal dust, mending and making do were part of a relentless routine in which the miner's wife could expect help only from her daughters, and by which her 'respectability' (and that of her family) would be judged. [**DOCUMENT I**] The woman was the fulcrum of the home as a unit: without her skills of household management many aspects of coalfield society, not least the ability of many men to throw themselves into trade-union and political activism, or of many more to countenance going on strike, might have been very different.

The price that women paid for this contribution to the functioning of coalfield society was high. Death rates for women aged between twenty and forty-four in the coalfield were higher than those for men, in defiance of the national average where the position was reversed. Repeated childbearing placed great strain on women, and poor long-term health was often the result. During the years of the Depression, commentators frequently remarked that women were sacrificing their own interests to those of their (often unemployed) husbands or children, going without food, and certainly without sufficient rest. Listlessness, anaemia, emaciation, poor dental health and premature ageing were all detected in married women and particularly in mothers. Maternal mortality rates rose in the coalfield throughout the 1920s, and by the 1930s female deaths from tuberculosis in the 15–35 age range in south Wales were 70 per cent above the England and Wales average, this rising to 250 per cent above in Merthyr Tydfil.

Relatively little is known about the state of relations between the sexes in the south Wales coalfield. No doubt the satisfaction to be gained from a state of matrimony varied widely from couple to couple. Certainly there were embittered and violent relationships from which women found it difficult to escape, given the general absence of economic opportunities and the culture of social disapproval that descended on the divorced and separated. Equally there were happy marriages, more often than not characterized by a husband's capacity for earning regular wages, his avoidance of alcohol in anything but moderate quantities, and his concern not to 'bother' his wife with sexual demands that would most likely lead to unwanted pregnancies. (Coal-mining areas throughout Britain exhibited high, if falling, levels of fertility in this period.) In between these two extremes were varying degrees of fulfilment and estrangement, with opportunities for companionship, let alone romance, often marginalized by the daily grind of hard manual labour for both parties. No doubt in some marriages the woman did have the upper hand, but most variables militated against this. The 'myth of the Welsh Mam' has been rightly criticized for attributing to miners' wives a degree of power they did not possess. In handing over his weekly wage packet to his wife (after deducting or being given a certain amount to cover beer, cigarettes, newspapers and other 'pocket-money' items), the miner was not bowing to her superiority or control as much as passing on the responsibility for household budgeting, which could often involve seeking out credit, pawning, buying on hire-purchase, or simply going without. Shopping was very much the preserve of wife, not husband. The woman may have had power over the home, but the limits to that power were set by a deeply patriarchal economy and society.

Outside the home, women's opportunities in all spheres were decidedly limited. Many forms of popular leisure were heavily gendered: the public house, the club and the workmen's institute were all, formally or informally, largely male domains. [**DOCUMENT XV**] In any case, the long hours of labour in the home that were required of miners' wives ensured that women with families had very little leisure time, enjoyed few if any holidays, and found their main outings only in the form of shopping trips and occasional attendance at the local cinema. The cinema, along with the wireless and, for some, the church or chapel, were the major forms of leisure pursuit for women in the coalfield. Each was largely passive and included an element of escapism, although both the cinema and religion did provide opportunities for socializing and access to some sort of relatively common cultural experience. The most important dimension of women's lives outside the home, however, was that of the wider family and friends in the neighbourhood, who could provide networks of mutual support that sustained them in times of trouble.

Coalfield society, then, was deeply fractured along the line of gender division. South Wales was, predominantly, a patriarchal society in which women occupied a subordinate, though far from insignificant, position. Only in the long term, beyond the scope of this work, would an economic shift, bringing a far greater percentage of women into the paid work-force, begin to undermine the strict demarcation of women's and men's 'worlds', and to create the social and cultural space in which coalfield women could start to exercise control over their own lives.

An appraisal of ethnic divisions within the south Wales coalfield must begin with an appreciation of how, from the mid-nineteenth century onwards, the society had been formed not only through natural population increase, but more importantly by waves of inward migration, initially overwhelmingly from elsewhere in Wales, but later from England and other places too. A study of the population census of 1911 for the Glamorgan coalfield indicates that whilst 47 per cent of the total in-migrant population of the county had been born in Wales (including Monmouthshire), 49 per cent had been born in England and the remainder in Ireland, Scotland and elsewhere. The proportion of English-born in Monmouthshire (excluding Newport County Borough) stood at 59 per cent, that of Welsh-born 33 per cent. What was still in the process of formation in the early twentieth century in the south Wales coalfield was a society of mixed, largely English and Welsh, origin. [**DOCUMENT II**] It was also a society which was moving with some rapidity towards being English in language. Although there were widespread differences between individual valleys and townships, the percentage of Welsh-speakers (monoglots and bilinguals) in Monmouthshire fell in this period from 13 per cent in 1901 to 6 per cent by 1931 and to 4 per cent by

1951. In Glamorgan the decline was from 44 per cent in 1901 to 30 per cent by 1931 and 20 per cent by 1951. Only in Carmarthenshire did Welsh remain a language that could be spoken by a majority of people, although here it also fell from 90 per cent in 1901 to 82 per cent by 1931 and 77 per cent by 1951; it is also significant that the percentage of monoglot Welsh-speakers in the county fell from 36 per cent in 1901 to 9 per cent by 1931 and 4 per cent by 1951. County figures mask the greater strength of Welsh in the Valleys than on the coast, at least in Glamorgan, where 57 per cent of Merthyr's population and 55 per cent of Rhondda's were Welsh-speaking in 1901, but even here the decline was dramatic enough: down to 40 and 46 per cent respectively by 1931, and to 25 and 29 per cent in 1951, with very few monoglots being recorded in either area after the First World War. Although the size of the total Welsh-speaking population is significant for assessing the rapidity and dynamics of language decline, an appreciation of how coalfield communities functioned is best gained by considering what proportion of the population was able to speak English, as local codes of language use increasingly required that English was the spoken medium in formal public gatherings such as trade-union and political meetings, and English was predominantly the language of the mass-circulation popular press.

English-born migrants came preponderantly from the west and south-west of England, particularly the counties of Gloucestershire, Herefordshire, Somerset and Devon. The evidence for twentieth-century ethnic tension between the indigenous Welsh population (a term that, in any case, cannot be applied unambiguously to Monmouthshire) and English in-migrants is very small. In part this is due to the decades of in-migration that had already taken place, and in part to the fact that language barriers were broken down with the spread of English as the universal medium. With the linguistic transition from Welsh to English regularly taking place within families, group antagonisms were unlikely to coalesce around linguistic or cultural identities. In the more westerly parts of the coalfield, in the anthracite district, there is evidence that in-migrants learned Welsh at least up to the First World War, though how long this process went on afterwards is unclear. Hostility by some towards inexperienced workmen being taken on at the mines, or towards the ideas of trade unionism and socialism might have been occasionally clothed in the language of cultural difference, but their origins were in the competition of the market-place, be it for labour or for ideological loyalty. Both were short-lived phenomena, as the solidarity that was necessary for effective trade unionism and the collectivist principles of the labour movement united workers irrespective of birthplace or linguistic capacity. [**DOCUMENT XX**] Significantly, Frank Hodges won the miners' agency in the Garw Valley before the First World War despite being an English-born English monoglot when all other candidates for the post could speak Welsh, and Merthyr-born English monoglot Arthur Horner repeated the experience in the Gwendraeth Valley twenty years later. Although some of those who observed and wrote about the problems of the coalfield believed that they could distinguish between 'the old-established Welsh stock' and 'foreign' elements, and accorded this distinction significance in the spread of 'economic and social theories and policies which would appear to cut across Welsh tradition', this was progressively belied by the increasingly prominent industrial and political role adopted by the most homogeneously 'Welsh' part of the coalfield, the anthracite area. By the end of the period considered in this book, although there was still much linguistic diversity across the coalfield, its people of both Welsh and English origin had come to share in an essentially similar self-image.

The experience of other ethnic groups within the coalfield may not have been so comfortable. The Irish had had a significant minority presence in the Valleys during the nineteenth century, but anti-Irish violence had systematically driven them out of particular areas, and those who remained seem, by and large, to have become integrated in the trade-union and political structures of the majority. Also integrated, though rather later, and not without teething troubles, were the few hundred Spanish families which came first to Dowlais and then to Abercrave.

Both the Irish who remained in the coalfield and the Spanish worked in the coalfield's heavy industries, but this was not true of the other two ethnic groups to leave their mark in south Wales. At the beginning of the twentieth century there were many small and scattered Jewish communities in the Valleys (sustaining a total of nine synagogues and three cemeteries), and although there were Jewish miners, most Jews worked as pawnbrokers, clothiers, jewellers, butchers, bootmakers, tobacconists or furniture dealers. Such businesses were the initial (though not exclusive) focus of serious rioting that took place in the Sirhowy, Ebbw, Rhymney and Aber Valleys in 1911. Probably of greater long-term significance in driving Jews from valley communities was the Depression of the 1920s and 1930s, which ruined many small businesses, and led many Jews to migrate from the coalfield and towards the coastal towns.

The last ethnic group large or visible enough to warrant mention is that of the Italians, of whom there were over 1,300 in Glamorgan and Monmouthshire by 1921, and whose lasting cultural contribution was the 'Bracchi' shop or café. There were over 300 of these in Wales, mainly in the south, by the mid-1930s, providing an attractive and cheap non-alcoholic alternative to pubs and clubs. There were occasional instances of ethnic tension: a Bracchi shop was attacked during the Tonypandy riots of 1910, and when Italy entered the Second World War some Italian shops in Aberdare and Tonypandy were also targeted, and all Italian men were interned in what was a serious over-reaction on the part of the authorities. But by and large the Italians of south Wales made a welcome contribution to the cosmopolitan society they joined.

The last dimension of ethnic divides in the south Wales coalfield is a religious one. In the nineteenth century friction between Welsh-speakers and English in-migrants had often derived from competing demands on the question of worship; Catholic and Jewish groups also sometimes found themselves singled out, ostensibly at least, on the ground of their faith. There is much anecdotal weight attached to the importance of chapel and church loyalties, in politics, leisure and education. However, the experience of twentieth-century secularization seems to have contributed to a marked diminution of the significance of these tensions.

To obtain a reliable estimate of the proportion of the population that regularly attended a place of worship in the region is extremely difficult. Membership figures available for individual churches indicate a constant decline in the first half of the twentieth century. In the Cynon Valley, membership of the four Congregational churches fell from over 2,000 in the first decade of the century to just over 1,000 by the early 1950s. Membership of five Baptist churches fell from 1,700 to under 800 between 1925 and 1955, and of all Calvinistic Methodist churches from just under 6,000 to under 1,400 between 1922 and 1949. Of equal significance was the collapse in the numbers of *gwrandawyr* ('listeners' or adherents rather than actual members) attached to the churches. At the beginning of the century most Nonconformist churches had at least twice as many *gwrandawyr* as members, but by the Second World War most had disappeared. This is not to suggest that religious organizations did not remain important in coalfield society as a whole, but it is likely that a majority of the population were no more than very occasional attenders at any place of worship. One estimate in the Eastern Valley in the late 1930s was that no more than a fifth of the people went to church with any regularity. [**DOCUMENT XXI**]

The implication of such a decline in religious attendance for an understanding of social divisions is that any internal structuring of the population of the coalfield that may have taken place along lines of denominational loyalty or religious-inspired 'respectability' was likely to be less prominent towards the end of the period than it may have been at the beginning. It has been suggested that, in areas where the Welsh language was at its strongest, chapels may have retained a higher proportion of their members than in Anglicized areas and that, for some, the break from both Welsh and Nonconformity was part of the same social shift. None of this, however, suggests any exacerbation of social cleavages. There is considerable evidence to suggest that the chapel and the public house did not appeal to discrete constituencies in the mining valleys, regardless of the pious rhetoric of ministers or the irreverent excitability of brewers. Religion did not become irrelevant to coalfield society and continued to play a key part in the composition of its image, but its social leadership was on the wane, largely displaced by the secular hopes of the labour movement. Its contribution to the relatively low level of ethnic tension that existed in the coalfield was slight.

The third fault-line along which coalfield society might have divided, particularly in the inter-war years, was that caused by unemployment and poverty. By 1928 the south Wales coalfield had acquired the reputation of a 'distressed' or 'depressed' area, and the persistent commissions of inquiry and social surveys that had taken its industrial militancy as their focus now switched to investigating the economic remedies for unemployment and its social ramifications. There is no doubting the seriousness of the malaise: by 1930 unemployment in Glamorgan and Monmouthshire was running at 28 per cent, and rose to 41 per cent by 1932. Although the rate slid back to the mid-thirties throughout most of the rest of the decade, for many families this represented a massive human disaster. However, to assess the impact of unemployment on the cohesion of coalfield society we need to take into account more variables than those of county averages. For a start, there was great variation between settlements in the coalfield in the scale and nature of the unemployment experienced. A survey in 1937 revealed that whilst Brynmawr suffered 57 per cent and Ferndale 56 per cent unemployment, Resolven and Tumble in the anthracite coalfield escaped with only 5 per cent and 13 per cent respectively. The anthracite area had an unemployment level at this time below the national average. Even within the central and eastern parts of the coalfield there were areas such as Bargoed (20 per cent), Ogmore Vale (22 per cent) and Blackwood (24 per cent) which were escaping the worst of the storm. Generally the blackspots were at the heads of the Valleys, from Merthyr to Brynmawr, and in these areas well over half of all miners might have been unemployed at one time or another during the 1930s. To take the Nantyglo and Blaina area as an example, seven out of the nine collieries had closed there in 1921, inaugurating more than a decade and a half of economic depression and social hardship. Between 1921 and 1935, 70 to 75 per cent of the male population was consistently unemployed, and the overall population fell from 16,488 to 12,550.

Of equal significance to the local incidence of unemployment was its duration. Although periods of short-term unemployment, lasting from a few days to three months, were undoubtedly very inconvenient and imposed considerable strain, not least because the work patterns imposed by colliery companies sometimes resulted in maximum disruption of unemployment benefits and a net financial loss for some colliers, they were less socially alienating than the consequences of long-term 'idleness'. The extent of this varied from valley to valley: short-term unemployment was a more common experience in the Garw and Rhondda Valleys, for instance, than in the heads of the Valleys communities. Across south Wales as a whole in 1935, about a fifth of the unemployed had been out of work for less than three months, but over half had seen no work for over a year, and a year earlier it had been estimated that, west of the Vale of Neath, over half had been out of work for more than two years.

The long-term unemployed tended to be drawn mostly from the higher age groups, of thirty-five years and over, which were sometimes displaced or disadvantaged by mechanization; considerable anxiety was expressed by government inspectors that as the spell of unemployment lengthened, so they would become unfit for any future work whatsoever. Many of the worst worries as to the unemployed becoming apathetic and listless seem to have been unfounded: in Blaina, for instance, where there had been 1,176 registered unemployed in August 1937, there were only six by April 1942, owing to the regeneration of the economy during wartime.

Bearing in mind that there was no stereotypical 'unemployed miner', only an 'intense variety', many different pursuits and activities were engaged in by those with unwelcome time on their hands. For some it was the garden or allotment that occupied them, for others a chance to hone their carpentry skills, or to take strolls on the mountainsides. Local sporting events could still be followed with reduced admission prices for the unemployed, and the cinema proved cheap enough for an occasional visit. A minority, perhaps an eighth of the unemployed, joined one of the 200 or more unemployed clubs that were established by voluntary movements and local authorities across the coalfield, where they could learn new, if not always directly useful, skills and 'put the world to rights'. For others, the National Unemployed Workers' Movement provided both fellowship and a chance to air grievances, whilst more miners were probably found still taking advantage of the workmen's institutes and libraries, access to which they enjoyed through being unemployed members of the SWMF. This scheme allowed the unemployed to participate in union benefits whilst paying considerably reduced dues. Yet others found sociability in the familiar faces to be regularly encountered queuing at the unemployment exchange. None of this is to deny that being unemployed was a severe trial and a highly undesirable alternative to full-time employment. But what it does indicate is that the unemployed were not likely to be wholly set apart from the rest of society, particularly in a society in which they might be the majority, and in which most of their fellow workers had experienced unemployment at one time or another. Such evidence of social exclusion as can be found relates either to individuals who became withdrawn or experienced tensions within their own families as a result of unemployment, or to those who discontinued attendance at church or chapel for want of clothes deemed suitable for the occasion. On the whole, however, the unemployed reflected the values, for better or worse, of the communities of which they were a part.

The strongest evidence of social division arising from unemployment and poverty emerges not from changed behavioural patterns in coalfield society, but from the levels of out-migration and poor health that can be established for mining communities. It has been estimated that between 1920 and 1939 over 390,000 people left the counties of Monmouthshire, Breconshire and Glamorgan, representing a fifth of the 1920 population. Two-thirds of the out-migrants were under thirty, and it is no exaggeration to say that the coalfield haemorrhaged some of its future away during this period. These migrants went, overwhelmingly, to the new industrial towns of the south and the Midlands – to Oxford, Coventry, Watford and Slough – as well as to London and to Birmingham, and many contributed to the development of trade unionism and of the Labour Party in those areas.

As for those who stayed, by the end of the 1930s they were experiencing a mortality rate 17 per cent higher than the England and Wales average, and 31 per cent higher than that of the south-east of England. Benefits, savings, social support, local authority measures may have been enough to stave off widespread starvation amongst the unemployed, but they were insufficient to provide a decent diet that would produce healthy citizens. Standards of health were continually and insidiously undermined. Children in particular suffered from malnutrition, rickets, diphtheria and pneumonia, with a fifth of Merthyr children in the late 1930s dying before they reached their fifth birthday. In 1936, infant mortality was sixty-three per thousand live births in Glamorgan, compared with only forty-seven in the south-east of England. Deaths from measles in the coalfield were running at twice the national average, and maternal mortality rates were twice those of the south-east. Average life expectancy in Merthyr was forty-six and a half years in 1932, and 65,000 of the inhabitants of the coalfield died 'avoidable deaths', due to the impact of poverty upon health, in the decade after 1926. These figures are evidence of social division, but between the coalfield and the prosperous areas of 1930s Britain rather than within coalfield society itself.

One final indicator of social tension that may have been generated by unemployment and poverty is that of criminal activity. The inter-war years were a period of high levels of indictable crime in the coalfield, but this largely took the form of looting from coal trucks, the burglary of stores and offices, shoplifting, and the vandalizing of churches and chapels. Coal stealing accounted for half of all recorded indictable crime in Merthyr Tydfil in the 1920s, with young men and women the most regular culprits. Much of this activity had economic need at its root, but it was the colliery companies, the railway companies, merchants, shopkeepers and publicans who were the usual victims. Interpersonal theft and violence did occur but, in the main, rates of crime, as with the rates of disease, reflected a sense of external alienation rather than of internal rift.

The society of the south Wales coalfield in the period 1898–1947 was, then, something less than an organic whole providing mutual support and satisfaction to all its inhabitants. The most permanent and critical fracture was that of gender, which conditioned, and perhaps constrained, the lives of virtually every individual. Ethnic tensions were much less significant, and had a declining relevance to what was, increasingly and, on the whole, impressively, a cosmopolitan society. Possibly it was the serious threat to personal and social health represented by unemployment and poverty that helped to render ethnic attachments less meaningful than those of occupation, class and community. By the end of the period covered in this book, to be a citizen of the 'South Wales Coalfield' signalled a clustering of identities, economic, political, and social. 'South Wales' had found both a coherence and a significance that it was to retain long after the economic conditions of its emergence had melted away.

Notes

Chapter 1   Historical Perspectives
[1] Deian Hopkin, 'Reflections of an editor, 1972–87', *Llafur* 4, 4 (1987), 7.

Chapter 2   The Rise and Fall of the South Wales Coalfield
[1] Revd J. Vyrnwy Morgan, *The War and Wales* (London, Chapman & Hall, 1916), 291.

Chapter 3   The Industry
[1] Allen Hutt, *The Condition of the Working Class in Britain* (London, Martin Lawrence, 1933), 4.
[2] J. W. F. Rowe, *Wages in the Coal Industry* (London, P. S. King & Son Ltd, 1923), 117.

Chapter 4   Trade Unionism
[1] *Colliery Workers' Magazine*, 1, 4 (April 1923).
[2] South Wales Miners' Federation, *An Outline of the Work Accomplished on Behalf of the South Wales Colliery Workers* (Cardiff, SWMF, 1927), 3.
[3] Commission of Enquiry into Industrial Unrest, No. 7 Division, *Report of the Commissioners for Wales, including Monmouthshire*, Cd 8668 (London, HMSO, 1917), 17.

Chapter 5   Politics
[1] G. H. Armbruster, 'The Social Determination of Ideologies: being a study of a Welsh mining community' (Ph.D., University of London, 1940), 193.
[2] Gwyn A. Williams, *When Was Wales? A History of the Welsh* (Harmondsworth, Penguin, 1985), 271.
[3] *Colliery Workers' Magazine*, 3, 11 (November 1925).

Illustrative Documents

DOCUMENT I 'Miners' Town', B. L. Coombes, 1939

B. L. Coombes was a working miner who, in 1939, when living in Resolven, Glamorgan, published his renowned autobiography, These Poor Hands. *He wrote other books, articles and short stories throughout the 1940s and 1950s. This extract is one chapter of his* Fact *pamphlet,* I Am A Miner *(49–58).*

Line Street is typical of thousands of the streets that were built when collieries were started and there was no way of travelling quickly to work, so that the men had to be housed close to the colliery. They wanted houses at once and, apparently, were not particular as to what sort of houses they were. Of course wages were better then and the cost of living was lower, so there was always the chance that the miner and his family could break the monotony by going for a holiday. Those good days have passed for most miners, so they have to stay alongside the accumulation of generations of coal dust and slags – and have to leave the holiday-making to others.

One doctor stopped me recently at the top of the street and waved his arm to indicate the way he had come: 'There,' he stated; 'that's my idea of hell – a colliery village on a wet day.' Imagine a hundred houses built as a double row, all of grey stone, and with doors and windows that are painted the same colour by the painters employed by the company. If the woman is house-proud she polishes the door with one of the furniture polishes; if she is disheartened she leaves it alone. Have a weak electric lamp fastened to a pole at an average of one light to every thirty houses and allow about three paces square of coal dust to call a garden. Huddle these houses as tightly together as possible, then cover the slates and outside walls with a paste made from coal dust soaked with rain – and you have the outside of the sort of house that thousands of miners have to count as 'Home.'

Somehow, by slaving all their waking hours, the wives and mothers manage to defy the greyness outside and make the inside bright. They are painting and paper-hanging continuously, laying clean sacking on the floor to catch the dust from the homecoming worker, and replacing their valued mats when he has cleaned himself. They brighten their rooms with brass ornaments and are always cleaning and polishing – or hurrying along the passage to see whether that motor-car they can hear coming is the colliery ambulance or the bailiff's van.

Then, in about seventy of these houses put a second family in the front room as well, and in perhaps twenty of them put a third family. Add to the crowd of people a host of cockroaches which have been brought home in the pit clothes and which invade the rooms whenever the light is switched off. Have men coming into that stuffy house every eight hours and each man wet and coal-grimed. Have someone in the beds all day because when three shifts are worked some men must try to sleep by day, even when the children are playing in the passage. Have steaming clothes before the fire all day and night because the clothes must be dry for the men to return to work. If a woman had her husband and two sons working on different shifts she would need to be astir before five in the morning to get the one on the day shift off to work. Then the night-worker would return, the children would go to school, the afternoon worker would go to work, the day worker would return, then the night shift worker would have to get ready, and it would be past midnight before she had seen that the afternoon worker was fed and washed. The men could be left to tend for themselves I suppose, but most of them would fall asleep in their working clothes from exhaustion. Most mining women have feelings, and they will not let the one who is going leave the house unless they can see him start and wish him a safe return, for it may be the last time.

I like to stand at the top of Line Street on Friday and watch what goes on, for that is the only cheerful day of the week. Then Line Street, and the many people who are in it, have an alert air, for they are waiting the coming of the miners with the pay. At the upper end two greengrocers are waiting with loaded carts. Unnoticed by them, the pony of the one cart is sampling – and finding good – the apples on the other. A fish-and-chip cart is waiting to oblige those housewives who had not found the time, or inclination, to prepare the afternoon meal for the menfolk. A small group of tally-men and insurance collectors carry on a desultory argument near the corner, but reserve their energy and keenest persuasion for the rush that will soon start. A cockle woman – high-booted and short-skirted, with plaid shawl pinned across her broad bosom and a large white basket on her right arm – turned her face as far as the balancing of the wooden tub on her head would allow and smiled her greeting to the district nurse as she passed on her bicycle. Then a rattle of steel-shod feet on the rough stones in the roadway showed that the miners were coming. They came down the street in groups that became smaller when one turned in to his house or paused to greet a welcoming child. Almost every man had his pay held tight in his left trousers pocket whilst his right arm swung wide to assist his walking. Coal dust rose from their clothes as they stumbled over the stones; whilst their gleaming eyes, bright red lips and white teeth showing from black faces made them look like nigger minstrels. Each man had a tea jack in one pocket of his jacket and a food tin in the other. Some of them kicked their boots hard against a stone and took off their jackets outside their doors so as to avoid taking more dust inside than they could avoid. As the men arrived the 'chip' man poked his fire and stirred the potatoes in their boiling fat. His pony obeyed the command to 'git up, thar,' while he disturbed the afternoon with a scream of 'All 'ot. Chips, all 'ot.' The smell of his wares spread with the sound of his call.

This call brought several clean-aproned women to their doors. They waited – holding basins in their hands – hoping the men would arrive with the pay envelope before the chip cart reached them. Then the collectors became alert, lifted their cases, wished one another a dubious 'Good luck,' and started their rounds.

Afterwards, save for a procession of small children coming from the toffee-shops – usually the front room of a house – Line Street is calm for an hour or so, then there are hurried exits of housewives who have dressed themselves with care and carry a shopping bag slung over their arm and a satchel tightly held in their hand. It can safely be assumed that they have had a good pay and are going to the nearest considerable town at the end of the valley to get new clothes or to get the groceries for the week. They claim that the cost of train fare is more than regained by the extra choice of eatables and by the much lower prices that are charged in the town.

Half an hour before post time there is another procession, towards the post-office. These hurrying people carry coloured envelopes with printed names on them, and the bearers have the manner of people who have satisfactorily solved a difficult problem. The staff at the post-office is harassed by the demands for 'Shillin order, please,' or 'two sixpenny orders, please.' On the walls outside people are making mysterious marks on postal orders and licking the flaps of envelopes. We may work as hard as we can and risk our lives daily, but our only hope of affluence is by correctly guessing how many times a leather ball will hit the back of the net.

Very often the man who has a good pay that week cannot keep the good news to himself, nor can his wife. This does not make the other people living in that house feel any happier. The man may know that he has worked quite as hard as the other worker whose wife is flaunting the fact that he has brought home three pound ten or four pounds, yet his wife cannot pay what she owes and his children must wait for the boots they need.

On Saturday afternoons the football match is about the only excitement, and the rivalry between near-by villages is intense. The dayshift have to work the same hours on that day as any other, and in the middle of winter they have difficulty getting to the match in time. Many men go in their working clothes, and the touch-line shows a sprinkling of men with black faces and heavy boots. They are at an advantage there because anyone with clean clothes will not press too near, and there is always a danger that an enthusiast may involuntarily deliver the kick that he thought the player should have made, and pit boots are not soft when they come in contact with someone. I have seen men playing in football togs and with black faces; and very often the touch-line is marked with small coal. In any case it would be dangerous for men to bath in hot water and then shiver about on a football field on a cold day.

Saturday night comes – and the pictures. The news-reel shows us what is happening over the mountains that shelter and confine us from the outer world. We pay ninepence and sit on uncomfortable seats whilst our minds are lulled with happy-ending pictures. Occasionally we get a deal of amusement from the efforts of some producer to give a realistic picture of mining life. If we are single we take two one-and-threepenny seats in the gallery and from that position we hold hands in the semi-darkness and look down on the ordinary people below and the extraordinary people in the pictures. In the front twelve seats the 'kids' wait in a murmuring impatience for the arrival of a Western or a 'comick.' When either arrives they are subdued no longer.

It used to be the custom to replay the football game or to re-do the work of the week at the public house on Saturday night, then settle the inevitable disputes outside after closing time. Either the beer has become weaker or peace propaganda has had some effect, for we hardly ever go so far as raising our voices nowadays.

Sunday seems to be a day of parades. The sporty fellows hurry their dogs out for a walk, the cyclists speed away with lowered heads, the walkers collect their sticks and unbutton their shirts, and the more lethargic saunter along in groups and complain bitterly that 'one let me down in the short list,' or 'who would have thought that was the word of four letters as they wanted?'

Then comes the chapel parade, mostly men in the mornings. They have probably been ordered out of the way by the busy housewives. They hurry chapel-wards wearing dark suits and bowler hats, stiff collars and faces, and have an air of having forgotten the collection money. Before they have finished the service the first parade returns. This time dogs are following, at the limit of their leashes, and the walkers sniff as eagerly at the smell of cooking meat as they had inhaled the mountain air on the outward journey. Scarcely has the last dog been dragged indoors when the chapel worshippers are again on the streets.

Sunday afternoon is for the young people or for those who count themselves as competent to lead them. After Sunday School they parade along the roads, for the two main roads are the only way they can walk. The girls link arms and walk in a line, alert for mischief or adventure. The mining valleys have many things of which we must be ashamed, but childhood and young womanhood seem more beautiful here than anywhere else. The girls are mostly dark and very vivacious; they have a sense of dress and can speak and behave in a way that does their upbringing no discredit wherever they may be. The children are almost all cared for to the limit of their parents' ability; it is very rare that we hear of children being ill-treated here.

The women age early and become haggard, but the living conditions are responsible for that. One hardly ever hears anything of the Welshy accent that has been the butt of comedians – and is perpetuated in most of the BBC plays – in the mining villages nowadays. All the cultural activities, reading, singing and drama have developed the ways of the villagers, and it is unusual to hear anyone speak the half-English half-Welsh that is supposed to be the language of these mining valleys.

Sunday evening comes with its lighted and crowded chapels. The preachers are emphatic and the singing something to remember. We are like the negroes; we sing to let the world know our sorrows. Our hymns and songs are sad ones, in the minor keys, because we have little to rejoice over unless it is that we are still alive. I often think it would be better if we, and the negroes, lost our reputation for singing and gained one for action.

Almost the only crime, if you count it so, that happens in these villages is coal-stealing; and it seems strange that the men – or their relatives – who throw tons of coal into the gobs where it stays for ever, should be punished for taking a little waste coal. It is like a farmer punishing his workman for taking an apple that was rotting on the ground in a bumper season. When coal is too far from a roadway or there is not enough to fill a tram, it is packed back into the gobs or it may be thrown into a tram that is afterwards filled with rubbish. Coal with slag attached is also thrown into the rubbish trams. Many of these rubbish trams are taken outside and unloaded over the colliery tip – and these are eyesores in every mining valley. The unemployed, the widows, and sometimes the workmen, who have not had their coal from the colliery, come to these tips hunting for waste coal. Often they have to move a lot of rubbish and search diligently. If the coal was not taken that day it would be buried by the rubbish tipped during the next day and so they are only taking what would be wasted. These tips, however, are counted as private property and very often a policeman is waiting for a chance to justify his uniform; then a magistrate who has property of his own to protect shows his sympathy by fining the 'criminal' heavily – or perhaps sending him to gaol.

One wonderful thing has come to the coalfield since the Sankey Commission. I mean the welfare scheme which was financed by the levy of a penny a ton on all coal raised. We have institutes and libraries as well as parks as a result of this scheme. Often the welfare institute is the only place where one can go of a night if one has no money. Miners and their families seem to take naturally to acting in drama, and almost every village has its dramatic society and many have their drama week. Actors are plentiful and efficient, but good plays and the men to write them seem very rare. I believe the crowded conditions of housing make study or creative work of any kind almost impossible. I notice, too, that although the majority of us are ready to sing in a choir, and this type of singing comes easy to us, very few are prepared to study hard enough to become a real competent musician or a soloist. Again, it must be the conditions of living or the strain of very hard work that disheartens them.

There seems to be a great keenness for books, and queues are usually waiting for the library to open. Lack of money prevents the supply of books being kept up to date, and one has often to wait a long while for a special book from the circulating library.

Why was it ever allowed to reduce the welfare levy from a penny a ton to half that amount? It was doing so much good that it should have been doubled, not halved. I think that a photograph of Lord Sankey should hang in every one of these welfare institutes as some reminder of one man of another class who did understand and sympathize with the miners.

There is no one who can be counted rich in this area. The rich people who control our lives live at a considerable distance from here. So anyone who is in trouble can be fairly sure of help and sympathy. Everyone is interested in the injury or illness of another and the majority of houses are open-doored to anyone who may call. When a funeral happens, all who can possibly get there attend it, for as an old collier remarked, 'We'll all want somebody to carry us to the grave if we lives long enough.' The clothes we wear are not important; it is the respect that we try to show that matters.

DOCUMENT II 'Race, in-migration, language', 1917 commission

This extract is taken from the Commission of Enquiry into Industrial Unrest, No. 7 Division, Report of the Commissioners for Wales, including Monmouthshire, Cd 8668 (1917), 15–16. The authors of the report were Daniel Lleufer Thomas, Thomas Evans and Vernon Hartshorn, and the secretary was Edgar Chappell.

1. Race Admixture

During the last 50 years or so the rapid development of the coal mining industry, as also, to a less extent, of steel and tinplate manufactures, and the transport service, has attracted to this district exceptionally large numbers of immigrants from all parts of the United Kingdom, with even a sprinkling from beyond the seas. The resultant mixture of people in any particular district often presents great differences in their traditions and antecedents, in their speech, habits and temperament, in their mental and moral make-up generally. Until some 15 to 20 years ago, the native inhabitants had, in many respects, shown a marked capacity for stamping their own impress on all newcomers, and communicating to them a large measure of their own characteristics; of more recent years the process of assimilation has been unable to keep pace with the continuing influx of immigrants.

The Census statistics as to the birthplaces of the inhabitants, and of the language spoken by them furnish striking evidence as to the existence and extent of their racial and linguistic diversities. We should explain, however, that we use the expression 'racial' as a convenient term to indicate characteristics associated with different counties or provinces of the United Kingdom rather than with distinct races of people.

The following figures extracted from the last Census Returns show, for the Counties of Glamorgan and Monmouth, the proportion of the native to the immigrant inhabitants in 1911:

Table E. – Native and Immigrant Population

Of the enumerated Population, number born in	Glamorgan		Monmouthshire	
	Total	Percentage	Total	Percentage
County where enumerated	729,969	65.13	251,269	63.5
Other Counties of Wales (or Wales, but county not stated)	151,877	13.55	42,408	10.7
Other parts of the United Kingdom, colonies and at sea	215,940	19.25	95,079	24.1
Foreign countries	11,419	1.02	2,501	0.6
Birthplace not stated	11,705	1.05	4,462	1.1
Total	1,120,910		395,719	

It is thus seen that of the total population enumerated in Glamorgan and Monmouthshire in 1911, only 65.13 and 63.5 per cent. respectively were returned as having been born in the county where they resided. Other parts of Wales contributed 13.55 and 10.7 per cent. of the population of each of the two counties. About one-fifth of the population of Glamorgan and one-quarter of that of Monmouthshire were, however, English born or born outside Wales . . .

2. Rapid Growth of Population

A large proportion of the male immigrants are unmarried men; this is naturally so for it is the unencumbered man that can most easily migrate to a distance. In many cases, however, married men come alone, leaving their families at the old home. The proportion of females to males in the mining counties is consequently very low. Monmouthshire stands lowest of all the counties of England and Wales in this respect with only 912 females to each 1,000 males, Glamorgan comes next with 924, Carmarthenshire is sixth from the bottom with 987, and Brecknockshire eighth with 991 . . .

The full significance of such a state of things we cannot investigate, but the low proportion of females to males tends to increase the economic dependence of women in the mining community. On the other hand the high proportion of unmarried men and also of young men (whether married or otherwise) may to some extent account for the tendency to rash and impulsive action on the part of certain sections of the community . . .

3. Language

The linguistic conditions of the six counties of Wales which contain any considerable industrial population is also shown in the following table:

Table F. – Language spoken, 1911 (%)

County	Monoglot Welsh	Monoglot English	Bilinguals	Unknown or Foreign
Brecknock	5.45	57.1	36	1.45
Carmarthen	20.5	13.35	64.5	1.65
Denbigh	10.05	41.66	46.62	1.67
Flint	3.5	55.35	38.75	2.4
Glamorgan	3.07	58.9	35.03	3
Monmouth	0.41	86.27	9.25	4.07

Most of the characteristics both geographical and sociological hitherto alluded to – the physical configuration of the coalfield, and its racial and linguistic diversities – have a divisive effect on the population, and present obstacles to the growth of social solidarity. Even religion is able to produce less of the spirit of unity than might perhaps be expected. Apart from the long-continued conflict between the Church of England and Nonconformity, co-operation between the various Nonconformist bodies themselves is, on the whole, but spasmodic and confined to but few forms of common action, such as in connection with temperance, while the difference of language cuts clean across almost all denominations, separating those who habitually speak Welsh from the English-speaking people in the matter of religious worship.

Many of the immigrants, cut off from their old religious associations and other restraining influences, drift into indifference, and some flushed, with their larger earnings and freer life, into self-indulgence. Others are attracted by the more idealistic principles of socialism, while not a few of the more active spirits throw all their energy into the work of their trade union, aiming perhaps too exclusively at the merely economic welfare of their own class. In the life of the old-fashioned collier religion continues to play a large part; his pre-occupation with the affairs of his church or chapel, and his other-worldliness of spirit cause him to hold aloof from active participation in the work of his lodge or in trade union politics. Possibly the tone and spirit in which the business of the lodge is sometimes, or in some instances, carried on, might be distasteful to him, and, in former years, the fact of its meetings being held in licensed houses also proved a stumbling block. The ever-recurring non-unionist trouble is at least partly due to the constant influx into the district of immigrants, ignorant for the most part of the benefits, and unversed in the methods of trade unionism, for those who refuse to join are mostly newcomers drawn from agriculture or some other ill-paid or unorganised industry.

DOCUMENT III Unionization of south Wales miners, 1898–1947

This table has been compiled from the Digest *of Welsh Historical* Statistics *and from trade union membership files held in the Public Record Office.*

Year	Total employed	SWMF membership	% unionized
1898	128313	60000	47
1899	132682	104212	79
1900	147652	127894	87
1901	150412	124097	83

Year	Total employed	SWMF membership	% unionized
1902	154571	127435	82
1903	159161	125586	79
1904	163034	117097	72
1905	165609	110963	67
1906	174660	121261	69
1907	190263	135765	71
1908	201752	144580	72
1909	204984	141089	69
1910	213252	137553	65
1911	220887	116863	53
1912	225535	114208	51
1913	233134	153813	66
1914	234117	152112	65
1915	202655	135165	67
1916	214100	147089	69
1917	219718	158767	72
1918	218852	151806	69
1919	257613	185044	72
1920	271516	197668	73
1921	232215	117610	51
1922	243303	87080	36
1923	252909	147611	58
1924	250371	148469	59
1925	211254	129155	61
1926	217989	136250	63
1927	194260	72981	38
1928	168465	59858	36
1929	178530	74466	42
1930	172991	75480	44
1931	158271	62089	39
1932	145810	64138	44
1933	143014	63337	44
1934	139935	76949	55
1935	131855	85741	65
1936	126412	88379	70
1937	136088	101011	74
1938	134824	103322	77
1939	128774	108955	85
1940	128470	109538	85

Year	Total employed	SWMF membership	% unionized
1941	111649	96033	86
1942	114181	98179	86
1943	114274	103432	91
1944	112344	101222	90
1945	114900	96828	84
1946	115500	95949	83
1947	115500	101370	88

NB: Unemployed members are not included in the above totals.

DOCUMENT IV 'Combines and the workers', D. J. Williams, 1925

D. J. Williams, born in Gwauncaegurwen in 1897, was a miner and checkweigher, educated at Ruskin College, Oxford, and the Central Labour College; he sat on Pontardawe Rural District Council in 1931–45 and in 1945–64 he was Labour MP for Neath. He published Capitalist Combination in the Coal Industry *in 1924, and the following article was printed in the South Wales Miners' Federation monthly,* The Colliery Workers' Magazine *3, 1 (January 1925).*

The growth of these powerful Combines effects a complete revolution in the relations of Capital and Labour in the Coal industry. Time was when the Colliery worker knew his employer personally. In those days it was the custom of the owner himself to come round the faces to consider allowances, prices, special job rates, and to meet in person the workers and their representatives. Such is not the case now. The old relations of persons have given way to a new relation of things. The Combine is a vast machine, and the worker is merely a cog in it. He does not know his employers; probably he has never seen them. But the struggle between Labour and Capital still goes on, only it is now fought out in a more intensive form. It is now a struggle between the workers – through their Organisation – and the vast unit known as the Capitalist Combine . . .

Capitalism in the Coal industry to-day is not the Capitalism of the 19th Century. It is not the type of Capitalism which gave rise to modern Trade Unionism. Moreover, the Capitalism of to-day cannot be fought with the weapons of long ago: there is already far too much of this Don Quixotism in our Trade Union programmes. In order to cope with the new problems created by the development of new forms of Capitalist organisation, Trade Unions, as the industrial buckle and shield of the worker, should have their machinery constantly overhauled and renovated. Unless this is done, a Trade Union, as an effective fighting force, is soon rendered impotent and obsolete. Capitalism in the Coal Industry has recently gone through a series of revolutionary transformations, but the Miners' Union still tenaciously clings to its old, and in many respects out-worn, form of organisation . . .

The Combine carries to its highest form the power of Capital over Labour. There are innumerable instances of this in South Wales. Combines generally have a large number of Collieries under their control. When a strike takes place at one of these Collieries, the workers in the others are 'speeded up.' In times of a slump the Combine can close some of its Collieries and meet the restricted demands of the market from the others. Again, through its power over Labour, the Combine can make a wholesale attack on old customs and usages of the pits it takes over. In the Anthracite District there are some glaring instances of this policy of the Combines. Everywhere the development of Combination harshens the attitude of Capital to Labour, and intensifies the struggle between them . . .

Hardly any steps have been taken by the Miners to meet this new and ever-increasing danger. We still belong to a pre-Combine type of Federation. One thing is certain: if the Organisation is to justify itself, it will have to be brought into line with the changes that have taken place in the Capitalist side of the industry. Fortunately, there are signs that we are moving, though slowly, in this direction. A welcome sign of this is the development of the Combine Committee movement. It is early yet to estimate the significance of this. In so far, however, as it is a manifestation of a consciousness that new issues have to be faced, it is a most valuable indication. But it is not enough. Our Organisation as a whole is too loosely knit to meet the highly centralised and efficient power of the Combines. Take our Districts. No one will hold to-day that these are efficient fighting or even administrative units. They are, in fact, arbitrary geographic divisions; inevitable, at one time, it is true, but now nothing more than anachronisms.

The Collieries within them belong to different owners, often to different Combines; they offer no unifying force to bring the workers together; and in a conflict with the owners – a company or a

Combine – would stand no chance whatever. Certainly a new orientation is needed in Trade Union structure in South Wales. It is only too easy to say that we stand for the control of the Combines. Unless we take immediate steps to 'make the word flesh,' the Combines will control us even more completely than they do at present.

DOCUMENT V *The Miners' Next Step*, The Unofficial Reform Committee, 1912

The Miners' Next Step: Being a Suggested Scheme for the Reorganisation of the Federation, *was written by a small group of industrial unionist or syndicalist miners, the core of the Unofficial Reform Committee, centred in Mid Rhondda. This extract (16–20) is taken from chapter III: 'Workmen the "bosses," "leaders" the servants'.*

PREAMBLE TO MANIFESTO.

The present deplorable condition of the South Wales Miners' Federation calls imperatively for a summary of the situation, in an endeavour to discover where we stand.

The rapidity of industrial development is forcing the Federation to take action along lines for which there exists no machinery to properly carry out.

The control of the organisation by the rank and file is far too indirect.

The system of long agreements, with their elaborate precautions against direct action, cramp the free expression of the might of the workmen and prevent the securing of improved conditions, often when the mere exhibition of their strength would allow of it.

The sectional character of the organisation in the mining industry renders concerted action almost impossible, and thus every section helps to hinder and often defeat the other. What then is necessary to remedy the present evils?

PREAMBLE.

I.   A united industrial organisation, which, recognising the war of interest between workers and employers, is constructed on fighting lines, allowing for a rapid and simultaneous stoppage of wheels throughout the mining industry.

II. A constitution giving free and rapid control by the rank and file acting in such a way that conditions will be unified throughout the coalfield; so that pressure at one point would automatically affect all others and thus readily command united action and resistance.

III. A programme of a wide and evolutionary working class character, admitting and encouraging sympathetic action with other sections of the workers.

IV. A policy which will compel the prompt and persistent use of the utmost cause of strength, to ensure that the conditions of the workmen shall always be as good as it is possible for them to be under the then existing circumstances . . .

PROGRAMME.

Ultimate objective

One organisation to cover the whole of the Coal, Ore, Slate, Stone, Clay, Salt, mining or quarrying industry of Great Britain, with one Central Executive.

That as a step to the attainment of that ideal, strenuous efforts be made to weld all National, County, or District Federations, at present comprising the Miners' Federation of Great Britain, into one compact organisation with one Central Executive, whose province it shall be to negotiate agreements and other matters requiring common action. That a cardinal principle of that organisation to be: that every man working in or about the mine, no matter what his craft or occupation – provisions having been made for representation on the Executive – be required to both join and observe its decisions.

IMMEDIATE STEPS – INDUSTRIAL.

I. That a minimum wage of 8/- per day, for all workmen employed in or about the mines, constitute a demand to be striven for nationally at once.

II. That subject to the foregoing having been obtained, we demand and use our power to obtain a 7 hour day.

PROGRAMME – POLITICAL.

That the organisation shall engage in political action, both local and national, on the basis of complete independence of, and hostility to all capitalist parties, with an avowed policy of wresting whatever advantage it can for the working class.

In the event of any representative of the organisation losing his seat, he shall be entitled to, and receive, the full protection of the organisation against victimisation.

GENERAL.

Alliances to be formed, and trades organisations fostered, with a view to steps being taken, to amalgamate all workers into one National and International union, to work for the taking over of all industries, by the workmen themselves.

The Programme is very comprehensive, because it deals with immediate objects, as well as ultimate aims. We must have our desired end in view all the time, in order to test new proposals and policies, to see whether they tend in that direction or not. For example, the working class, if it is to fight effectually, must be an army, not a mob. It must be classified, regimented and brigaded, along the lines indicated by the product. Thus, all miners, &c., have this in common, they delve in the earth to produce the minerals, ores, gems, salt, stone, &c., which form the basis of raw material for all other industries. Similarly the Railwaymen, Dockers, Seamen, Carters, etc., form the transport industry. Therefore, before an organised and self-disciplined working class can achieve its emancipation, it must coalesce on these lines.

It will be noticed that nothing is said about Conciliation Boards or Wages Agreements. The first two chapters will, however, have shown you that Conciliation Boards and Wages Agreements only lead us into a morass. As will be seen when perusing the policy and constitution, the suggested organisation is to be constructed to fight rather than to negotiate. It is based on the principle that we can only get what we are strong enough to win and retain . . .

Political action must go on side by side with industrial action. Such measures as the Mines Bill, Workmen's Compensation Acts, proposals for nationalising the Mines, etc., demand the presence in Parliament of men who directly represent, and are amenable to, the wishes and instructions of the workmen. While, the eagerness of Governments, to become a bludgeoning bully on behalf of the employers, could be somewhat restrained by the presence of men who were prepared to act in a courageous fashion.

DOCUMENT VI 'The mind of the miner', *Observer*, 1916

This article, the second of three examining 'The Mind of the Miner', was published in the Welsh Outlook *(August 1916), 246–8.*

The overwhelming majority of Welsh miners belong either to the Liberal Party or to the Labour Party. A small proportion of them in the Rhondda and neighbouring valleys have come under the influence of the Conservative clubs, but the number is almost negligible, and there is no hope of the Conservative Party securing any safe seats in South Wales mining areas. There are two schools of Liberals: those who desire to be represented by middle or upper class people – lawyers, merchants, or 'gentlemen': and those who desire representation by Trade Union nominees. The former school, now a rapidly diminishing section, are hostile to Labour representation, and object to Trade Unions being levied for political purposes. The latter desire Labour representation, but wish their representatives to work in close co-operation with the Liberal Party. This section, also, is diminishing in numbers and influence. The Liberal-Labour men are impressed by the fact that during Trade Union disputes Liberal employers are equally as antagonistic to the men as Conservative employers, and they cannot believe that men who are industrially opposed to them can be good political allies. This contrast has been strongly emphasised by the propagandist ILP, and during recent years Liberal-Labourism has largely been replaced by Independent Labourism. The movement towards independent Labour representation has been to some extent handicapped by the fact that the most strenuous advocates of the new method have failed to take national sentiment into account. The candidates put forward on behalf of the Labour Party have often been men who cannot speak the vernacular, and Welsh-speaking Liberal champions have been able to win and hold the seats by playing upon national feeling. The official Liberals have also had the strong support of Nonconformist preachers, in whose minds the Disestablishment of the Anglican Church in Wales has dominated all other political issues. Latterly the Labour Party have become wiser political strategists, while the power of the preacher in politics has been considerably weakened. Liberal candidates, in order to retain their seats, are now obliged to declare themselves in favour of measures which a few years ago they would have regarded as ultra-revolutionary. The policy of independent Labour representation at present commands the support of a considerable majority of the miners, but it must not be assumed that the miners are therefore whole-hog Socialists. Many of the older men accept part of the Socialist programme of the ILP, even though they may not be connected with that organisation. A very much larger proportion of the young men have come under ILP influence, and it is these who constitute the driving force in the industrial and political Labour movement in the South Wales coalfield. The strength of this force cannot be measured by Parliamentary votes. The Trade Union constituency is not co-terminous with the political constituency. The latter consists of householders only and includes people of all classes. The Miners' Federation constituency comprises, in addition to married miners possessed of parliamentary votes, a large body of young unmarried men to whom the political suffrage has not yet been extended. It is from the ranks of the latter that the ILP draws the bulk of its membership, and it is these young men who have imbibed to the greatest extent the revolutionary proposals of the Socialists. The young men decide industrial issues; the older men political issues. The young men determine the choice of Parliamentary Labour candidates, but they do not yet have a voice in electing them to Parliament. The decision of a Federation ballot does not always accurately forecast the decision of the Parliamentary ballot. In the recent Merthyr contest Mr Winstone, the official Labour-Socialist candidate and member of the ILP, beat the anti-ILP candidate, Mr Stanton in the Federation ballot, but was himself hopelessly beaten in the Parliamentary fight.

The future, however, is with the ILP. The granting of manhood suffrage is bound to strengthen the ranks of the Labour Party, and to lead to the extension of Socialist opinion throughout South Wales. This is a period of transition. During the next few years the miners will accept political objects which will be closely allied to the industrial aims of the Miners' Federation. The ever-growing hostility of the miners to capitalism is bound to find expression in politics, and the time may not be far distant when every parliamentary constituency in the coalfield will be held by a Federation nominee professing advanced Labour-Socialist views.

DOCUMENT VII Vernon Hartshorn, before the Sankey Commission, 1919

Vernon Hartshorn (born in 1872 in Cross Keys, Monmouthshire) was, successively, miner, checkweigher, miners' agent, and eventually president of the SWMF(1922–4). He sat as Labour MP for Ogmore in 1918–31, and was Postmaster General in the first Labour government in 1924. In March 1919 he gave evidence to the Royal Commission on the Coal Industry (the Sankey Commission), which was considering, inter alia, the nationalization of the mines.

Now what the miners say is this: Having regard to the arduous and hazardous and unpleasant nature of their calling, they consider that they are rendering a useful service which places the public under an obligation to ensure to them a decent civilised existence in return for those services. I think you may take it that the miners will no longer consent to be regarded as mere hands whose chief function is to produce profits for idle shareholders. They will insist upon being regarded as useful public servants, and to be treated as such. I think in that respect, or on this point, I might just say that whatever is done in the matter of an advance in wage, or a reduction of hours, at the present time, resulting from this inquiry, unless the mines become State owned we shall certainly have a very serious situation in the mining industry. I think State ownership of the mines has become inevitable. At the present time the miners are in the frame of mind in which they are prepared to treat and deal fairly and to recognise all the interests that have grown up in the industry. But I am perfectly certain that, unless the demand for State ownership is conceded at the present time, Syndicalism, or, if you like, Bolshevikism, will take the place of the demand being put forward by the miners at the present time. Now none of us want that. I am sure everyone representing the miners in the capacity of leaders, at any rate, is anxious that the change shall take place without any unfairness to any of the interests that have been developed in the industry. Of course we quite realise what we always say about the profiteering of the colliery owners, but there are a large number of people who have devoted their money and genius and experience in a sense to the service of the community, the same as a miner has. A large number of them have invested their money in it on the understanding that the State would treat it as a proper investment, and we do not want to alter that. We want them to be fairly treated. But I think I am only stating an actual fact when I say that, if this is not conceded at the present time, a movement will develop among the miners which will take a different form from that of nationalisation. I assume that colliery owners, on the other side, know exactly what I am referring to. They have experience of its development in each of the coalfields to-day, and I think it is in the public interest and in the interests of everyone connected with the industry that a real and determined effort should be made to put the mining industry on a basis of State ownership. I do not know that I desire to say more than that at the moment in connection with the general aspect of things.

DOCUMENT VIII Will Paynter, 1969

Will Paynter was born in Whitchurch, Cardiff, in 1903, but moved to Trebanog, Rhondda, in 1914. He worked as a miner and checkweigher until victimized; he was a member of the Communist Party from 1929, and a full-time organizer from 1931 to 1936. From 1936 he was a member of the SWMF Executive Committee and became miners' agent in the Rhymney Valley in 1939. He was president of the NUM (South Wales Area) in 1951–9, and general secretary of the NUM in 1959–68. He was interviewed in April 1969 by Hywel Francis and David Smith (transcript of interview held in the South Wales Miners' Library.)

When did you first begin to get involved in politics?

Well, in politics . . . I don't know, you say the nineteen twenties . . . the characteristic of the nineteen twenties was one of massive confrontations between the employers and the workers in Britain. And both in nineteen twenty one and in nineteen twenty six, the miners that were chosen you know, for the first round of attack, locked out for three months in nineteen twenty one, and I remember . . . you see before nineteen twenty one, you had the demobilisation of the soldiers from the army following the first world war, the pits were actually saturated with manpower, because I think there was a serious fear of revolution in Britain. You know there had been, not only the Russian revolution, Soviets and Workers Councils had been established in a lot of countries in Europe. The Sankey Award I believe is a symptom of the fear that the ruling class of Britain had at that time. And so, we were, how shall I say, in a general way, concerned with politics. Politics became part of the conversation. I remember when I was a kid of about sixteen, during the nineteen twenty one strike, discussing revolution as youngsters you know, because it had happened in the Soviet Union, because there was all this ferment. The strike was on, there was discussion, you know, about stopping the pumps, flooding the pits you know, the kind of discussions. Well that led into the nineteen twenty-six, first the General Strike, then we were out, we went out on May 1st, I didn't get back to work until December of that year. So the whole character of the situation, where the employers were attacking the, because every time there was a wage reduction, and they were substantial wage reductions. It was almost impossible to, not to, if you were thinking at all, to arrive at the conclusion that there was something wrong with society. And it's really during the twenty-six strike that I first became positively interested. I was attending the meetings, A. J. Cook and a lot of other people speaking. I think my concerns then were more with the issues that were involved in the strike probably than with politics. But after the twenty six strike, I had to back to work nights, which meant I broke with my pals, they were working days, and I took to reading. Cymmer Library had, probably one of the – Arthur Horner acknowledges, probably one of the best selections of literature that you'd find in any library in the Rhondda, and they were good libraries, the old miners institutes in the Rhondda, you know. Fiction, serious stuff and philosophy. I gradually gravitated to sociology. I sort of read myself to social democratic writers, to Dietzgen, Marx, Engels you know they had a marvellous selection of books. Groping, there was no sort of design in the kind of reading, I suppose I read a lot more books than I had any need to, sort of wandering through it. And finally reached the conclusion that, well, let's put it this way, I reached the conclusion from reading, that I couldn't accept that the Labour Party was a socialist party, that it hadn't or never would, take the people of this country to socialism, and I still hold that view too. The only Party that I saw that represented the sort of conclusions that I was reaching was the Communist Party. Well I didn't join the Communist Party immediately I reached this position, and that was largely due to the situation at home. As I say, my mother was very religious, and my sister here was an Apostolic, both she and her husband had been to India as – you'd call them Evangelists I suppose. So the religious and the sort of absolutist sense, that's the background of the family. I was never an absolutist in that sense, I suppose I went two years to chapel, and I reached the conclusion that religion was – didn't explain anything, you know. I went to chapel for about two years, purely out of a sense of duty to the – well, not prepared to make the break in the family, because of the upset it would cause. So I had to break those shackles really before I became attached to any political organisation.

DOCUMENT IX *Portrait of a Mining Town*, Philip Massey, 1937

Philip Massey was a political journalist who wrote Portrait of a Mining Town, *a study of Blaina and Nantyglo in Monmouthshire, based largely on interviews with local inhabitants, for a* Fact *pamphlet. This extract is taken from chapter 2: 'Opinions' (39–42).*

The district has been traditionally Labour since the end of the War. Before and during the War, Trade Union leaders were generally regarded as extremists politically. After the War the Labour Party obtained power locally on a programme of social services and made big improvements in this respect. There is no general understanding of the meaning of socialism; the average man votes for a working-class candidate who will try to get something for the workers and against a ruling class candidate who won't. The vast majority of Labour leaders are ex-Trade Union officials or existing Trade Union officials, who more or less automatically became political leaders when Labour's chance came. There is considerable discontent with local Labour leaders, as a result of which some people go Communist and some revert to a sort of Liberalism; the mass continue to vote Labour but are politically apathetic. A specific ground for discontent is the level of the Public Assistance rates paid by the County Council; surprise was expressed at County Councillors denouncing the Unemployment Assistance Board; a number of people considered that they got better treatment from the latter. It is a little difficult to see where the Labour leaders of the future are – the majority of the young men are apathetic and of those that are not apathetic a number are Communists or Communist sympathizers. Most of the members of the Communist Party are between 25 and 40 years old. Communism is regarded by most people as a ginger movement – useful to buck up the Labour leaders – or even as a means of organized personal attack and exposure of 'scandals'.

The Labour Party has a very large Trade Union membership, and a considerable volume of steady support from the wives of Trade

Unionists. It works principally through the Trades and Labour Council, which consists of delegates from the Lodges and other Trade Union branches, the three Ward Labour Parties and the three Women's Sections. Unemployed miners retain their membership through the Unemployed Lodge (1d. a week). The fortnightly Trades and Labour Council meetings are well attended, for it is there that the important business is done, Urban District Councillors and County Councillors for the district reporting to the delegates who then report back to the Lodges. Every Trade Union member can thus keep in touch – but attendance at Lodge meetings appears to be generally less than 10 per cent. of membership; at the Unemployed Lodge lower still; though it is vastly higher when a vital issue is to be discussed.

Ward Labour Party meetings, of individual members, are held monthly, sometimes more often, in the winter; these do not obtain a large attendance – say 40 to 60 or so – there are not many individual members. It is a common complaint from those holding more radical views than those of the Party leaders that these meetings are caucuses. It is open to anyone who wants, of course (except a Communist), to become an individual member, but it seems to be considered that an attempt to buck up the leaders through the Ward Parties would fail because of the considerable reserve of loyal members who would come if there was organized opposition. On the other hand the low attendances at Lodge meetings are pointed to as a sign of either contentment or apathy.

At public meetings held by the Labour Party the attendance may be from 100 to 400 or even more, depending mainly on whether current political issues are vital to the mass of the people, and on the nearness of elections.

Support for the Labour Party is therefore based mainly on certain concrete advantages obtained in the past and consequent expectation of more in the future (though this will be difficult in view of the poverty of the area) and on tradition and the view that the Labour leaders are experienced and know what the people want. There is a further factor of considerable importance – the willingness of Labour councillors to help people fill in forms and generally to assist in regard to little matters of difficulty which arise. There seems to be little doubt that many Labour leaders owe much of their support to creating a personal sense of obligation by their willingness to assist in this way, and a common ground of criticism is that they will promise to 'see to things' for an individual, rather than challenge on the principle involved, thus creating a feeling of indebtedness.

The district may therefore be said to be a Labour stronghold by results, but there is not much active rank and file movement behind it. This arises in part from the lack of effective opposition. The Communist Party has about 35 members in Nantyglo but its voting strength is out of all proportion to its membership.

DOCUMENT X 'A dream comes true', 1947

This newspaper article discussing the nationalization of the coal industry was written by 'G.R.', a columnist with the weekly Rhondda Leader, *and published on 11 January 1947.*

Somewhere about the first years of the present century a branch of the Independent Labour Party was formed at Porth, and this writer went to report the event for this paper. The chief speaker was Mr Noah Ablett, and the subject discussed was the nationalisation of all the means of production, distribution and exchange. In a few months a live organisation became established at Porth, and among the speakers was Mr C. B. Stanton, afterwards MP for Aberdare. The first speech Mr Stanton made dealt at length with the need for the nationalisation of the mines. With a voice which carried from the soap-box upon which he was speaking at the entrance to Cymmer Colliery yard, to the whole of the Porth Square, the picturesque Charlie Stanton, his great head of long hair waving about, told a crowd of listeners of the enormity of the coal mines being owned by private individuals and companies and of the unspeakable advantages which would accrue from their ownership by the State. From those early beginnings until last week that theme became a rosy vision, a dream of great days to come. Speaker after speaker dealt with it, and no miners meeting of any importance passed without prophetic references to the vision of the days of post nationalisation of the mines. And now that dream has come true. For a week the men have descended the pits that now belong to the Nation. To some the results are somewhat of an anti-climax. Nothing has happened. The pit is just as deep and the face of the coal is as far in. There is as yet no lessening of the work or any decrease in the dust and its menace. Will there be any more coal raised? Will the stain of absenteeism be removed in whole or in part? The whole of the world's worry and suffering and anxiety of all classes of the people over the need for coal could be wiped out – or if as Mr Shinwell has told us if it could only be reduced to an average of 11 per cent. No body of people could do so much for so many people throughout the world as the men who have now found their own dream come true. It would be the crowning argument in the present government's case for a nationalisation of the Nation's great services.

DOCUMENT XI 'When a man is an efficient collier', 1933

The anonymous prize-winning essay from which this extract is drawn was published in the Ocean and National Magazine, 6, 5 *(May 1933).*

There has been, during recent years, a gradual speeding up process at the coal face, due to the shortening of hours of the shift. A certain output of coal must be maintained, and to achieve this, a greater proportion of the collier's time must be spent at the coal face producing coal. *This has been responsible for a great loss of pride in the collier's work.*

When his hours of labour were relatively long, and his output restricted, he had considerable time to drive wide roadways with good height. This he did for his own benefit, because he could build his tram of coal to hold a few more hundredweights, to counteract the restricted number of trams. To-day, his number of trams is unlimited, and he does not take such pride in good filling as he previously did.

To-day, a collier will stop and admire a tram of coal well filled, and pass a poor one without comment; but years ago the reverse was the case, because good filling was then commonplace.

The same applied to his roadway and coal face. He could spend more time in packing properly, and timbering. His deadwork being unlimited within reason, he removed all broken timbers from his roadway and erected new ones. Any rubbish falling in his roadway he either walled up neatly, or took to the face for packing. Real pride was taken in practically all he did, and heated were the arguments as to who had the better road, and who was the better collier! That phase has unfortunately passed, but the collier is not entirely to blame for it. The great pity is that the craftsmanship of the past generation is not being properly taught and handed down to the coming one. There is a ray of hope, however. The modern method of steel ringing, which demands adequate height and width of straight roadway; steel props which demand good packing for their successful use; and trams of greater capacity which demand good roadways, may revive that pride which is gradually being lost.

DOCUMENT XII *Ups and Downs*, Walter Haydn Davies, 1975

Walter Haydn Davies was a Bedlinog miner turned teacher, and published two volumes of autobiography and reminiscence. This is taken from his second, 220–7.

Often have I heard elderly miners refer to one particular show-cards occasion which had serious consequences for it led to a strike. The usual notice had been posted in the checkweigher's office as well as on the miners' notice board near the Lamp Room, stating that on a given day 'show-cards' was to take place: those employed at the colliery were expected to bring their Federation cards with them to be checked by the Lodge officials. That day the 'show-cards' revealed that there were three non-Unionists, Llew Bollocks, Huw Hen Gownt and Ianto Half-time, and that a dozen or so miners were in arrears with their contributions. The latter promised to pay an extra six-pence with their weekly contributions until their arrears were cleared. But the three non-Unionists were obdurate and would not give their promise to join the Union. They could not see that they were in any way indebted to the Union for the improvements that had taken place in working conditions and the general standard of living. 'A good workman does not want a Union to fight for his interests because a good workman will always get his due reward for honest endeavour,' they argued; they insisted that the Unions merely safeguarded the 'lazy buggers' and those who practiced ca-canny. In exasperation Twm Dwywaith, the Union leader, retorted that to try to persuade them to join the Union was like applying medicine to the dead; he threatened other means would have to be adopted to force them to see reason, and warned them that he would report to the mass-meeting of their fellow miners that moral persuasion had been useless.

Pay day arrived, and these recalcitrant individuals made no attempt to pay their Trade Union subscriptions. The Lodge officials then engaged the services of the village's 'town crier', Dic Crys Gwyn, to go forth with his bell to announce that a mass-meeting of miners employed in the Bedlinog Colliery would take place the following Monday. This was well attended. The Chairman of the

Lodge emphasised that Union support had already resulted in stronger bargaining power, and better working conditions and living standards ensued. It was clear that the three recalcitrant non-Unionists felt no sense of moral obligation but were content to thrive like parasites on the growing strength of the Union. They must now be forced to see reason, and he moved, 'that there should be a stoppage of work on the following Wednesday, and that all members of the Federation should assemble at the coalyard at a given time so that they could march as a body to the homes of the offenders.' This procedure was agreed and a committee to organise the procession and to consider the methods to be adopted at the homes of the offenders was selected.

Great was the excitement at the coalyard on the day of the procession. The Lodge officials were there in force, supported by members of the village band, and those who were to carry the banners. On one banner was inscribed, 'Unity is Strength, M.F.G.B.', on the other 'United We Stand, Divided We Fall', and on the third 'Keep Stanton on the job.' This reference to Stanton was made because at that time he was one of the most militant of miners' leaders in South Wales. Among the crowd were a number of collier boys who sported frying-pans and tin tommy boxes. Eliab Owen, the Lodge Chairman, a stickler for organisation and discipline when anything took place under his authority, enquired why these accessories were necessary. Up spoke Dai Twm, saying, 'We thought banging the empty tommy boxes outside the houses of the non-Unionists would make them see that they were prepared to take the very food from our mouths.' So piercing would be the ring that it would be sure to give one of them, Llew Bollocks, not only a headache but a belly-ache.

'I see sense in that,' said Eliab, 'but what about the flaming frying-pans?'

'Oh,' said Dai Twm. 'Huw Hen Gownt is sure to swear when we are outside his house that he will settle pay-day. But we all know a promise by him is made to be broken – for his motto is 'Hen Gownt talu byth' (Given credit, never pay). But if he swears on oath he'll pay up, touching the frying-pan as he does so, he'll be afraid to go back on his word because he'll sizzle in Hell as the fat does in the frying-pan when it is on the fire!'

'Yes,' chimed in Willie Stories, always ready with a yarn, 'it is not the first time a frying-pan has been used instead of a Bible; when there was a strike at Powell's Level in Llancaeiach many years ago the manager was made to swear on the frying-pan that we would never again employ strike-breakers. No Bible was available at the time so the frying-pan was considered to be the next best thing.'

'Ay,' remarked Eliab, 'I remember hearing that these blacklegs were frightened out of their wits by the booing and jeering of the men, women and girls in the crowd who also beat kettles and frying-pans together. I hope we'll be able to make a similar frightening din to beat these three non-Unionists into submission.'

The members of the Lodge committee had by now assembled the crowd into some kind of order so that they could march in procession four abreast through the village to the houses of the non-Unionists. Eliab blew a loud blast on his whistle, for the band was ready. Banners fluttered joyously in the breeze, and the crowd began marching at Eliab's commanding shout, 'By the Left, Quick March!'

Away they went, along Moriah Street, over the bridge, past the Colliers' Platform, and down the hill, the band playing 'The British Grenadiers', the schoolboys lining the pavement singing lustily a wishful parody that the prevailing hot air would create breeze enough to cause Llew's discomforture [sic] and embarrassment in the lower regions. As they neared Llew's house, the procession halted after a moment to allow the band to switch to a tune of more significant tempo, 'The Dead March'. Outside the house the band ceased playing, and Dan the Band transferred his steady beat from the big drum to Llew's front door. As he did so a number of the crowd began hissing like geese and the youngsters made merry hell with their banging of tommy boxes and frying-pans. Such was the din that Llew's wife, Blod Sgrech, screamed blue murder. Jones the Bobby was seen scurrying down the Co-op Field, but keeping well in the background, hiding behind the wall. Blod's screaming was nothing new to him because it occurred regularly on Saturday nights, when her husband, the worse for drink, gave her her weekly hiding. Llew, like Jones the bobby, kept from view and it was Blod who appeared at an upstairs window to trumpet forth that Llew would 'pay up, on pay-day.'

Fully satisfied with Blod's assurance Eliab blew his whistle, the crowd again assembled in marching order, and away they went, marking time to the band's playing in quick tempo, this time to the tune of 'Onward, Christian Soldiers.' On they marched towards the Square, calling on the way to Huw Hen Gownt's residence. It was anticipated that Hen Gownt would be the hardest of the three nuts to crack. He went through life blissfully convinced that his accumulated debts would inevitably have to be written off. Extreme intimidation was the only answer to his obduracy.

'Let's give him some Scotch Broth!' shouted Dai Twm.

Eliab replied, 'Scotch Cattle, you mean. You know what miners calling themselves Scotch Cattle did to the blacklegs at Nantyglo many years ago? To frighten these scabs into submission the members of the Union calling themselves Scotch Cattle, blackened their faces and marched to the houses where the blacklegs lived and smashed the windows, destroyed the furniture and beat up the occupants, then for good measure they used red paint to draw the face of a bull, and on its horns painted the hearts of the blacklegs, writing underneath, "We hereby warn you that we are determined to draw the hearts out of you and fix them upon the horns of a bull; so that everyone will see the fate of every traitor"!'

A yelling crowd demanding payment was a new experience for Huw. Packmen could be duped into making second calls, a bum-bailiff could be side-tracked with a meal and a noggin; but this was assault en masse. The hissing of the crowd, the din of the tommy boxes and frying-pans unnerved him. But breaking point came with the painting of a gory bull's head (which was more like that of a devil) on his front door resulting in his solemn promise as he touched the largest frying-pan that he would be a member of the Union. In addition was the assurance from his wife, Sarah Anne, that she would see that the money would be in the Treasurer's hands next pay-day even if she had to sell Huw's milgi (greyhound) to get the cash to make full payment.

Eliab's blast on the whistle was a joyous one and the procession marched gaily down the Cwm to call on the third non-Unionist Ianto Half-time. He proved easy meat. This shiftless, beer-drinking, skittle-playing bachelor had already been threatened with eviction by his militant landlady if he didn't hand over his Federation dues. One knock on the door and he meekly complied.

Such instances were typical of the coalfield in those days. It was a period when the Trade Unions were being fused into powerful bodies, and the allegiance of the miners to their Union, the South Wales Miners' Federation, had to be made as strong as it was to their chapel. This became so, thus helping to develop in them a marked class-consciousness. They then sought not only Heaven in the hereafter, but in the present, and it was the Union that would be the saving grace. The mass-meetings the miners held in the Workmen's Hall had at times the atmosphere of religious revival within Chapel walls. But it was the idea of the show-cards which brought most sinners to their knees. It was a very simple procedure in itself but proved extremely effective.

The show-cards practice did much to encourage a high percentage membership of the South Wales Miners' Federation. This was helpful, for a strong organisation was vital in the miners' case in a rapidly expanding industry in which new seams of coal were being developed and new price-lists were continually being negotiated. On the success of such negotiations, after all, depended the livelihood of the miners. This meant that unity was vital, as the banner the miners displayed revealed the phrase 'Unity is Strength' inscribed thereon. On marches such banners were proudly displayed like the battle honours of soldiers – rightly so, the Union having won many a battle for them. Indeed, their organisation was more to them than a Benefit Society – it was a commune, a part of the fabric of their very lives. Woe betide anyone who attempted to weaken the solidarity of the Federation and the spirit of community it symbolised . . .

To the miners, such transgressors against their will were sinners, and at mass meetings which were held on Squares and in the Miners' Institutes there prevailed an atmosphere remarkably like that of a sitting of a commune during the French Revolution period. The show-cards demonstration was the non-Unionists tumbril whilst social ostracisation was the blackleg's lot, the former a very simple and sometimes gay procedure involving little lasting bitterness, the latter resulting in a sore that never healed. As no man wished to be brought to such shame, even the weakest links became so welded as to strengthen the Union's aim to improve the lot of the miners as a whole.

DOCUMENT XIII 'Labour on the council', Iorwerth Thomas, 1935

Iorrie Thomas was born in 1895, and was a miner and checkweigher in Cwmparc, Rhondda. He served on the Rhondda Urban District Council in 1928–52 (chairman in 1938–9), and sat as Labour MP for Rhondda West in 1950–66. This article was published in the Rhondda Clarion: The Official Organ of the Rhondda Borough Labour Party, *1 (September 1935).*

The advent of the Labour Party to the position it now holds upon the Rhondda Council is an accomplishment that registers one phase of the general advance made by the working classes towards self-government. To attain a majority of Labour members has meant years of hard work and involved much sacrifice. Years ago it was customary for working classes to take all their troubles to the family butcher, grocer, or local tradesman. Spiritually and temporally the working man placed all his faith on somebody else. He would go cap in hand to somebody else in the village to appeal and invite Mr Somebody to represent him on the Council. If we examine the composition of the Council during these days, we would discover that it was a collection of tradesmen, colliery managers, and solicitors, etc. As the result of propaganda in the pioneering days, working men and women were persuaded to have faith in themselves and not put their trust in others.

Gradually the idea of independent working class representation took root. Eventually working men from the coal face and women from the home were returned to the Council, until finally we gained power. The purpose of the activities that will appear in this paper each month will be to show how working men and women organized under the banner of the Labour Party have utilized the machinery of government in the Rhondda for the benefit of the workers of the Rhondda. We shall educate you about the problems of local government. We want you to understand the work of the Labour Party. Its plan and policy, etc. We want to convince you that working men can govern. As an example of Labour's record, let us quote the efforts made to assist the unemployed. Let it be clearly understood here that the Labour Party realises that unemployment can only be eliminated by the abolition of Capitalism. But we cannot wait and bray until this capitalist system collapses. We must do something now for the suffering people of the Rhondda. The Rhondda Labour Council has done excellent work for the unemployed in the provision of work schemes. Since 1923 we have spent on Rhondda work schemes about £450,000. This has provided employment for 70,000 man weeks, approximately 5,400 men working for a period of thirteen weeks each. We have in hand for the coming winter additional work schemes for the unemployed. The Labour Party has submitted proposals for relief work amounting to £315,000, which would provide work for 49,000 man weeks or work for 4,000 for a period of thirteen weeks each. We anticipate that during this winter we shall put into effect work for which we shall have gained from the Commissioners over £100,000. Included in this will be provision for three new swimming baths. In conclusion we take pride in the fact

that our Council is to the fore in its endeavour to do something
tangible for the unemployed and not merely shout about it.

DOCUMENT XIV Cyril Gwyther, 1949 and 1989

*Cyril Gwyther was a Methodist minister at Central Hall, Tonypandy, in
1935–47. The first extract is taken from his* The Valley shall be Exalted:
Light Shines in the Rhondda *(1949), 71–2; the second from an
interview conducted by the present author at the Revd Gwyther's home in
Pembroke Dock in 1989.*

(a) In my early days, I once invited Mr George Davey, a shrewd and
sagacious student of social life, to tell me the distinction between
Socialism and Communism as seen in the life of the Valley. I was not
seeking a theoretical distinction – that was fairly clear to my mind –
but a practical one. He suggested that the distinction lay at this point
– Socialism captures the people of the Rhondda who are looking
'left,' but who believe in the pre-eminence of spiritual values, and
whose lives have been largely shaped by Christian influences.
Communism makes it appeal chiefly to those who deny the validity
of the spiritual and believe in economic determinism. Broadly
speaking, the distinction is sound. The Labour Party in the Rhondda,
advocating Socialism, is largely made up of people whose approach
to social and economic problems is along religious and idealistic
lines. Many of its leaders are well-known members of the Churches;
in many cases they are lay preachers. With the Communists, this is
not so. Their approach is definitely materialistic – as they would
quickly tell us. I am not suggesting that the Communists of the
Rhondda are not appreciative of the finer qualities of life. I have
friends who claim to be Communists. I have often noticed their zeal,
their complete refusal to acknowledge defeat, the wholehearted way
in which they work and sacrifice for their cause. Even though the
membership of the Party is comparatively small, it is well chosen and
disciplined. You are not welcomed into the membership of the Communists because you happen to be 'a nice fellow,' or because 'you
play a good game,' or even because you are mildly interested. You
become a member when you are convinced that Communism is the
economic solution of the world's need.

(b) I would say the majority of them [members of the Labour Party] were men who had some kind of attachment to the church or chapel . . . I'm not suggesting that everybody in the Labour Party went to church or chapel on Sundays but they had, shall I say, a religious background, a religious interpretation of life . . . These men who formed the Labour Party, who approached the situation along, shall we say, idealistic and ethical lines, were not reactionaries, and they were not a whit behind those who were more revolutionary. They were just as sensitive to the iniquities of the time, and all the injustices of the capitalist system, just as active and volatile in their lives; but their approach, they had a certain background, a certain foundation, their approach was always along the lines of persuasion and consensus, more than using force . . . I would always like to emphasise that as I knew the situation in the Rhondda, the Labour Party was as much alive, and just as much opposed to the system of capitalism, as the Communists. The Communists hadn't got a monopoly of zeal.

DOCUMENT XV 'Women in the Labour movement', 'Matron', 1912

'Matron' was a regular columnist responsible for 'Our women's column' in the Rhondda Socialist Newspaper, *being the BOMB of the Rhondda Workers. This article appeared on 21 December 1912.*

How many women who have worked in factory or workshop, or who have served their time as a working man's wife, brought up a family on a working man's wage, and therefore know the struggle, are leading in the Women's Labour Movement? The Women's Labour League, founded to benefit working women, is a case of the women of the middle class bending to help women of the working class. All the names of women prominent in the Labour Movement are women who have come into the movement out of sympathy, and not out of a real experience of the working woman's needs and strategies. They are not women of the working class.

There is something to account for this difference between the Labour Movement as evolved by men and the Labour Movement as evolved by women. The lower economic position of working women partly accounts for the position. These women cannot afford to pay secretaries, agents and leaders to give their time to organisation, etc.

These upper class women step in; they have money and leisure to bestow, and they do the work gratuitously. But if working class women are ever to be anything else than a subject class, they must work out their own social and political salvation from within. This is particularly true with regard to the wives of working men.

While progress is being recorded all round, they are still in a primitive state of domestic slavery. Knowledge is wanted, enlightenment, a new hope, that they may begin to see their way to make changes in their domestic affairs which will bring them to more hum and sweeter conditions of life.

It is with the position of these working class wives in the local Labour Movement I shall now deal. There are five bodies which at present represent the local Labour Movement: (1) The Central Labour College Classes; (2) Branches of the ILP; (3) Trades and Labour Councils; (4) Lodges of the Miners' Federation; (5) Urban District Council.

Labour Classes

The educational classes of the Central Labour College are formed for men and women. How many women are attending these classes throughout the valley? They are few, if any. As to the cause, I do not believe it lies in any mental incapacity in the women to understand the subjects dealt with, or in any deep disinclination on their part to try and improve their minds. Most of the attendance at these classes is due to the personal influence of one man upon another. How much persuasion has been extended to women? Has any encouragement been given them to attend, or has cold water been thrown over any little enthusiasm they might have had?

ILP Branches

These are conducted almost with a total disregard to the existence of women in the district or to matters in which women are interested. How many women members are there in the valley? Where are the wives, daughters and sisters of the men who run affairs? Are the women wanted as members? Whether or not, they are needed in order that a serious attempt may be made to grapple with the evil social conditions.

The Lodges

A smile will arise at the notion of a collier's wife attending a lodge meeting, and yet how much of what is settled there involves the lives of the women. Have men any moral right to settle matters which concern the lives of women as well as their own without consulting the women? There are times and occasions when an open meeting of the lodges could be held, and the women concerned consulted in matters.

Trades and Labour Councils

As these bodies are constituted it seems an impossibility for any working woman to become a member thereof. A shop girl, teacher or domestic servant of a Trades Union may, but the whole class of wives are debarred from any activity through these bodies. I have the rules of one of these Councils which are so formed.

Urban District Councils

With all these avenues of labour activity partly or entirely closed to women the obvious absence of women from this public body causes no surprise. It is impossible for any woman to be chosen for election by the organisations which hold the strings. Women of the leisured and wealthy classes are limited, even if their sympathies were Labour, and they elected to run as independent candidates. What is needed to make the Labour Party on the Council genuinely representative of the people is one or more women of the working class, whose interest is not the result of pity from a distance, but the effect of life's contact with working class conditions. It is exceedingly difficult for an individual, however keen, to accomplish any social work as an individual; but united with others of similar aim much can be achieved.

I should like to make an appeal for the women . . . It is this: 'It needs the men of the working class to help the women of the working class.' The women of the working class must be brought into the Labour Movement by their own flesh and blood.

DOCUMENT XVI Elizabeth Andrews, before the Sankey Commission 1919

Elizabeth Andrews, born in Hirwaun in 1882, worked as a dressmaker and settled in the Rhondda Valleys in 1908. She married a local socialist, Thomas Tye Andrews, and became the Labour Party's women's organizer for Wales in 1919. She submitted the following evidence to the Sankey Commission in May 1919.

I am the wife of a miner [corrected by Mrs Andrews in person to 'ex-miner'], and many of my people are engaged in the mining industry. I have lived all my life in the mining areas, and as a member of the Women's Co-operative Guild, and of the Labour Party, have had many opportunities of discussing the conditions with other women.

Housing

Women acquiesce in bad housing in Wales because they have no alternative, under the present circumstances due to the extreme shortage of houses, a shortage which was very acute in industrial areas long before the war. The statement made that women acquiesce in bad housing because they like low rent I strongly resent on behalf of the women, as they have had to pay a very big increase in rent this last ten years for the same houses and conditions. I quote Rhondda, for example, being one of the largest mining areas in Wales.

Population: 165,051 (1918 estimate)
Number of inhabited houses: 28,384.
Number of miners: 44,460 (estimate).
The estimated need for houses at present is 1,500 to 2,000.

Houses that have been condemned before the war (not fit for human habitation) are still occupied owing to the shortage, and most of them occupied by large families. The reason is that most landlords will not rent their best houses to people who have large families. The overcrowding of these cellar dwellings are to a great extent responsible for the high infantile death-rate of 103 per 1,000.

Pithead Baths. – This reform like all other reforms at first met with opposition owing to the fact that it would bring a change in customs, and naturally would meet with prejudice. But a revolution in ideas among the miners and their wives has taken place since then. This question has been discussed at public meetings all over South Wales during the last 18 months, and especially this last five months it has become the question of the day. It was the women of the Rhondda who renewed this agitation by asking the Executive of the South Wales Miners' Federation to urge the lodges to take the matter up, and correspondence took place in the South Wales daily papers which has aroused the interest of the miners' wives all over the coalfields. Conferences are to be held at various centres to press forward the campaign. I have addressed 25 meetings since March in mining areas in South Wales, where this question of pithead baths has been fully discussed, and both men and women have realised what it means to them in raising the standard of life all round, individually in the home life, and in municipal life. Unsightly workmen's trains and cars would be done away with, and the miners could then travel in cleanliness and comfort. Pithead baths would reduce the physical strain on the mother caused through lifting heavy tubs and boilers. A midwife of 23 years' experience in the same district in the Rhondda stated to me that the majority of cases she has had of premature births and extreme female ailments are due to the physical strain of lifting heavy tubs and boilers in their homes which they had to do under the present housing conditions.

DOCUMENT XVII 'What I think of life' (*circa* 1938)

This was written by an anonymous 36-year-old married woman with one child from the Pontypool area, and was reproduced in G. H. Armbruster, 'The social determination of ideologies: being a study of a Welsh mining community' (Ph.D., University of London, 1940), 261.

1. I am quite satisfied with life but not with the surrounding of which we have to live, as we have not suficient to live on and the conditions of our home make us full discontented we would like to have more children to make our happiness complete but our circumstans wont let us as during the period of pregny I know I could not get the things I would require in the way of extra foods and clothing that we as mothers requre.

2. Do I desire a change?:
    Yes I do desire a change. Of better housing accomadition and nurseing homes for us to bring our children and also a higher

wage for my husband as we would be more happier and contented in our home. I think this thing can be brought about by the Labour movement.

3. I am Labour through the influence of my husband. Finding that my duties at home as denied my chances to visit any meetings it just means to me that being denied of the faccalities of going to these meetings and I have to rely upon my husband as a guide in this matter.

4. What would I consider a satisfactory wage is about £4 a week as I could get suffent food and clothing and also a little spending money.

DOCUMENT XVIII 'Phyllis', 1996

'Phyllis' was born, one of twelve children, in 1913 in Tylorstown, her father a stoker in No. 9 pit. This extract is from an interview conducted by Rosemary Scadden in March 1996, to be found in ' "Be good sweet maid; and let who will be clever": A study of Welsh girls in domestic service during the inter-war period' (M. Sc. Econ. (Women's Studies), University of Wales, Cardiff, 1996), 129–30.

My mother was a very hard worker, a very hard worker. She took in a lot of washing. She did washing for a grocer and his son, which meant the white coats and the white aprons. She took in lodgers, she did everything you had to do for lodgers. It was a big house, four bedrooms, big living room, kitchen, back yard. Well she used to do all that.

She was very good with her meals. She was excellent baking her bread, Christmas cakes. The smell of Christmas cakes when we used to fetch them from the bakehouse, for Christmas! She'd make about seven. When she made bread she made about seven loaves of bread. We would have to go down the bakehouse, my brother and I, to bring them up. You know the crusts would be hanging off these and we'd be dying to take the crusts off, but she was a strict mother. But she wasn't cruel in any way. She was very strict because being young boys and girls, growing up, she always had her eye on both sides, all the time.

She had the old tubs there for washing and the scrubbing boards. She would take in that washing and do her own washing, which was a lot . . . The cooking then was the old fashioned fireplace, where the ovens were by the side and the hobs and the brass rod around the fire place, the big heavy kettle. Every Sunday she would make tart, all in the oven, by the fire. We always had good food, nothing fancy. She'd make a huge iron saucepan, brimming to the top, with stews, dumplings and all that. What was really good food, porridge in the morning. A big saucepan full of porridge to go to school. Then we would come home teatime, she'd have something for us then – cake for our tea, salad or something like that. Supper time it was just a bit of bread and butter or a couple of biscuits to go to bed. We had to be in bed early. She didn't like us out late at all.

Did she have anyone to help her with all these chores, or just you children had to help?

We weren't really old enough to do a lot. But my older sister did help a lot, to look after us. She nursed some of the younger ones as they were still babies. As she was getting a bit older, she was going out and help mothers that were having babies. So she was doing all the heavy work that is done on confinement. When she was out on those things it would be either my other sister, or myself.

We were always squabbling over the housework. My older sister, she had to do the big middle room, my other sister had to do the back kitchen, with the flagstones – whiten the hearth and the cleaning of the fender, scrub the flagstones, then sprinkle sand over the back kitchen. Then in the middle room it was tiles and the rugs. We used to make the rugs between us, save all the old pieces of coloured rags, get a piece of sacking and sometimes there would be two of us or three of us with a peg and we'd make lovely coloured rugs. Imagine then, they had to be cleaned and shaken out in the yard, before you could put them back. My sister, had the privilege of doing the middle room which had the lovely fire place and the hob, with the black lead – it always had to be polished with a piece of velvet. That would shine up like glass. The fender there was steel so that was done with Brasso. Everything was to shine by the fireplace.

Did you use the middle room?

We lived there. We used both rooms, the living room and the back kitchen, as we used to call it, yes. We used to mainly eat, if there were less of us, in the back kitchen. Especially on a Sunday, when we'd all be in, in the middle room. Again then, as I said, my sister had the privilege, I thought at the time. My younger sister could do the back kitchen and my older sister the middle kitchen, but I had to do the passage and all a long flight of steps outside. I didn't like it at all. I wanted to do the middle kitchen, but I never had the chance, so that was where I ended.

My mother was spotless, upstairs and downstairs. She had to go down a yard and up a garden, to where the line was, a very long garden. She had the four bedrooms of bedding, all in the tub and on the rubbing board and anything that had to be boiled – whites. They were boiled in an iron boiler, on the fire in the back kitchen, blued and starched – things that had to be starched. All the whites were blued, to come out lovely and white and then she'd take them down the garden and up the garden then, there was always the big line full. And we had nice weather, we seemed to have a lot of nice weather. You would have this lovely line full of washing blowing. Funnily enough my father used to go up and bring it in. I can always see him come back with a line full of washing.

DOCUMENT XIX *The Second Industrial Survey of South Wales*, 1937

The Second Industrial Survey of South Wales *was published on behalf of the National Industrial Development Council of Wales and Monmouthshire. The director of the Survey was Professor Hilary Marquand of the University College of South Wales and Monmouthshire, Cardiff. This extract is taken from a chapter in volume I on the distributive trades (Cardiff, 1937), 191.*

Substitution of female for male labour is prevented mainly by custom. There are a very large number of retail trades in which male assistants are employed almost exclusively – tailoring shops, grocers, butchers, fishmongers, men's hairdressers – to name but a few. There are some in which female labour is employed, usually under the supervision of males and there are some in which staffs of both sexes are employed. But it is quite evident that the trades in which male and female labour could be substituted one for the other are extremely few. Of the new retail trades which have very largely come into existence in the past ten years, 'wireless' shops employ men almost entirely. Men are usually employed in the 'club' trade. In the fixed price stores, female labour is employed entirely (but often under male supervision) and it is only there that we can trace substitution of male by female labour, although it is of an indirect nature. Such stores sell articles in competition with ordinary shops, some types of which employ male labour only – grocery goods are an example of such articles. There is in a similar way a certain indirect substitution of adult by juvenile labour. The practically new retail trade of women's hairdressing and 'beauty' shops is usually, but not always, staffed by women.

DOCUMENT XX *Brynmawr: A Study of a Distressed Area*, Hilda Jennings, 1934

Hilda Jennings's study of Brynmawr was based on the results of a social survey carried out by the Brynmawr Community Study Council between 1929 and 1932. This extract is taken from chapter IV: 'Origin and nationalities', 53–7.

The contemporaneous influx of Welsh and English immigrants which has been a constant feature in the history of Brynmawr, has persisted up to the present time. What have been the effects of the constant coming and going during the last century and a quarter? It is now almost impossible to ascertain in what proportions the Welsh and English stocks are present. Periods of industrial depression have caused emigration of the original inhabitants, while periods of sudden industrial development have brought in influxes of both Welsh and English workers. The effects of these influxes have to some extent been counterbalanced by the intermarriage of the young male workers with local girls, and in some cases the former have obtained a stake in the community by the acquisition of house-property by marriage. Assimilation of the newcomers has been helped in this way, and the community has set its stamp on English as well as Welsh inhabitants . . .

Students of the South Wales Coalfield have noted the marked capacity of the native Welsh population to impress their characteristics on newcomers from over the English border. In Brynmawr, as elsewhere in English-speaking industrial districts of South Wales, it is difficult to discriminate between the descendants of the original Welsh stock and of early immigrants from England. Certain physical characteristics persist, but in emotional tone and attitude to social, political and religious questions, the mark of the community is more apparent than that of the race. In the first generation of immigrants the fusion of traditions is often incomplete and the prior attachments to the original home may persist for many years. Obscurely seen yet none the less important, racial tendencies may be at work in their children and in the generations which follow; nevertheless, moderating or even running counter to these tendencies, are the influences of climate, scenery, local traditions, occupations and customs, all the attachments, standards and values which are common to the community and distinctive of it. Only indeed by the encircling atmosphere of a common physical and spiritual environment, can the paralysing effects of uprooting from the native soil and the sense of inner conflict and impotence which comes where allegiance to national cultures is divided, be counteracted. In the cosmopolitan industrial areas of South Wales, the community, as foster-mother, has a special part to play.

DOCUMENT XXI Mining town, 1942

In March–April 1942 the Mass Observation organization compiled a 'File report' (No. 1498) on the mining township of Blaina in the Ebbw Fach, Monmouthshire. In this extract (166) two descriptions of religious services in the town are provided.

1. The congregation in church on a fine morning in April, was very small, eighteen people, including two old men and four children, in one of the largest religious buildings in the district. Of the women, most were middle-aged or older, two were under thirty-five, and one girl was in her teens. The service, beginning at eleven o'clock, lasted barely three-quarters of an hour, and most people, leaving quickly, would have been home again by twelve. There was a small choir of not more than half-a-dozen people, but the tunes chosen for the hymns were not always easy to follow, and response from the congregation was unenthusiastic. Perhaps it was because the whole service was taken quickly and largely as a matter of routine, that people seemed not to be impressed. But there was also no attempt at emotional appeal in the sermon which, studied and thoughtful, appealed rather to the intellect of the congregation. This church sermon, however, stressed wider political issues and concentrated less on the question of personal salvation than did some of the sermons delivered in Blaina chapels in the same month.

The main theme of the morning's sermon was:

'Honour all men . . . In many parts of the world, and even among religious people, personality is at a discount . . . Man is made in the image of God . . . Jesus, by looking always for the best in people, helped them immeasurably . . . We have to learn afresh to look for the best, to recapture the Christian values, to emphasise the value of the individual.'

2. A chapel congregation in the evening of the same day, numbered five men, fifteen women and five children. (The building was constructed to hold at least two hundred). At this service, too, the congregation was mainly middle-aged, but there were a few young mothers with their children. The singing was good, full and unselfconscious, and the congregation was attentive to the service, and particularly to the sermon. The service was taken by a visiting deaconess who was an emotionally emphatic speaker and who succeeded well in linking together herself and her congregation, although the warmth of the response was offset by the small number present.

The text of the sermon was: 'There is no other name under Heaven whereby we may be saved' . . .

The sermon lasted nearly half-an-hour. When the service was over, people did not hurry off at once but stood about in the lobby of the chapel and on the pavement talking. Later, they joined the little procession of people who had been to evening service in other chapels and were now walking along Blaina high street, home.

Further Reading

Historiography and comparative perspectives

Huw Beynon and Terry Austrin, *Masters and Servants: Class and Patronage in the Making of a Labour Organisation: The Durham Miners and the English Political Tradition* (London, Rivers Oram Press, 1994). An interesting study indicating many common reference points with the culture of the south Wales miners.

Alan Campbell, Nina Fishman and David Howell (eds.), *Miners, Unions and Politics, 1910–47* (Aldershot, Scolar, 1996). An important collection of thematic and regional studies.

Roger Fagge, *Power, Culture and Conflict in the Coalfields: West Virginia and South Wales, 1900–22* (Manchester, Manchester University Press, 1996). A stimulating transatlantic comparison.

Gerald D. Feldman and Klaus Tenfelde (eds.), *Workers, Owners and Politics in Coal Mining: An International Comparison of Industrial Relations* (Munich, Berg, 1990).

David Gilbert, *Class, Community and Collective Action: Social Change in Two British Coalfields, 1850–1926* (Oxford, Oxford University Press, 1992). This combines a study of south Wales (Ynysybwl) and Nottinghamshire with more abstract thoughts on the concept of 'community' in mining areas.

Royden Harrison (ed.), *Independent Collier: The Coalminer as Archetypal Proletarian Reconsidered* (Hassocks, Harvester, 1978). A very important collection of essays, concerned to undermine the image of the miner as an 'archetypal proletarian'.

David Smith, 'The future of coalfield history', *Morgannwg*, 19 (1975), 57–70.

Klaus Tenfelde, 'The miners' community and the community of

Mining Historians', in Klaus Tenfelde (ed.), *Towards a Social History of Mining in the Nineteenth and Twentieth Centuries* (Munich, International Mining History Congress, 1992), 1201–15. Perceptive observations on mining history in an international context.

Jonathan Zeitlin, 'From labour history to the history of industrial relations', *Economic History Review*, 60 (1987), 159–84. A historiographical survey.

Economic history

Michael Asteris, 'The rise and decline of south Wales coal exports, 1870–1930', *Welsh History Review*, 13, 1 (1986), 24–43.

Trevor Boyns, 'Growth in the coal industry: the cases of Powell Duffryn and the Ocean Coal Company, 1864–1913', in Colin Baber and L. J. Williams (eds.), *Modern South Wales: Essays in Economic History* (Cardiff, University of Wales Press, 1986), 153–70.

Trevor Boyns, 'Work and death in the south Wales coalfield, 1874–1914', *Welsh History Review*, 12, 4 (1985), 514–37.

Trevor Boyns, 'Technical change and colliery explosions in the south Wales coalfield, *c.*1870–1914', *Welsh History Review*, 13, 2 (1986), 155–77.

Trevor Boyns, 'Rationalisation in the inter-war period: the case of the south Wales steam coal industry', *Business History*, 29 (1987), 282–303.

Trevor Boyns, 'Of machines and men in the 1920s', *Llafur*, 5, 2 (1989), 30–9. An account of technological change.

Trevor Boyns, 'Powell Duffryn: the use of machinery and production planning techniques in the South Wales coalfield', in Klaus Tenfelde (ed.), *Towards a Social History of Mining in the Nineteenth and Twentieth Centuries* (Munich, International Mining History Congress, 1992), 370–86.

Trevor Boyns, 'Jigging and shaking: technical choice in the south Wales coal industry between the wars', *Welsh History Review*, 17, 2 (1994), 230–51. This essay stresses the significance of conveyors.

Roy Church, *The History of the British Coal Industry*, vol. III: *1830–1913:Victorian Pre-eminence* (Oxford, Oxford University Press, 1986).

Martin Daunton, 'Down the pit: work in the Great Northern and south Wales coalfields, 1870–1914', *Economic History Review*, 34 (1981), 578–97. This looks at working techniques, and at the impact of the 1908 Eight Hours' Act.

Martin Daunton, 'Labour and technology in south Wales, 1870–1914', in Colin Baber and L. J. Williams (eds.), *Modern South Wales: Essays in Economic History* (Cardiff, University of Wales Press, 1986), 140–52.

G. M. Holmes, 'The south Wales coal industry 1850–1914', *Transactions of the Honourable Society of Cymmrodorion* (1976), 162–207. A survey article.

Graeme Holmes, 'The First World War and government coal control', in Colin Baber and L. J. Williams (eds.), *Modern South Wales: Essays in Economic History* (Cardiff, University of Wales Press, 1986), 206–21. This explains the staged nature of control.

Paul Jenkins, *Twenty by Fourteen: A History of the South Wales Tinplate Industry, 1700–1961* (Llandysul, Gomer, 1995).

A. H. John, *The Industrial Development of South Wales, 1750–1850: An Essay* (Cardiff, University of Wales Press, 1950).

J. H. Morris and L. J. Williams, *The South Wales Coal Industry, 1841–1875* (Cardiff, University of Wales Press, 1958).

J. H. Morris and L .J. Williams, 'The south Wales Sliding Scale, 1876–79: an experiment in industrial relations', in Walter E. Minchinton (ed.), *Industrial South Wales 1750–1914: Essays in Welsh Economic History* (London, Frank Cass & Co. Ltd., 1969), 218–31.

Barry Supple, *The History of the British Coal Industry*, vol. IV: *1913–1946: The Political Economy of Decline* (Oxford, Oxford University Press, 1987). An official history, none too sympathetic to the miners.

D. A. Thomas, 'War and the economy: the South Wales experience', in Colin Baber and L. J. Williams (eds.), *Modern South Wales: Essays in Economic History* (Cardiff, University of Wales Press, 1986), 251–77. The Second World War.

Rhodri Walters, 'Labour productivity in the South Wales coal industry', *Economic History Review*, 28 (1975), 280–303.

Rhodri Walters, 'Capital formation in the south Wales coal industry, 1840–1914', *Welsh History Review*, 10, 1 (1980), 69–92.

Rhodri Walters, *The Economic and Business History of the South Wales Steam Coal Industry, 1840–1914* (New York, Arno Press, 1977). This is full of relevant information.

John Williams (ed.), *Digest of Welsh Historical Statistics* (2 vols., Griffithstown, The Welsh Office, 1985). An exceedingly valuable compilation of historical statistics.

John Williams, *Was Wales Industrialised? Essays in Modern Welsh History* (Llandysul, Gomer, 1995). A first-class collection of essays, mostly on economic history.

Demographic, linguistic and migration history

Geoffrey Alderman, 'The anti-Jewish riots of August 1911 in south Wales', *Welsh History Review*, 6, 2 (1972), 190–200. An investigation of this curious episode.

Andy Chandler, 'The black death on wheels: unemployment and migration – the experience of inter-war south Wales', in Tim Williams (ed.), *Papers in Modern Welsh History* (Cardiff, Modern Wales Unit, 1982), 1–15. A very good study of the variable impact of unemployment and the demographic consequences.

Ursula R. Q. Henriques (ed.), *The Jews of South Wales: Historical Studies* (Cardiff, University of Wales Press, 1993). This volume includes chapters on the 1911 riots and on Jews in the valleys.

Colin Holmes, 'The Tredegar riots of 1911: anti-Jewish disturbances in south Wales', *Welsh History Review*, 11, 2 (1982), 214–25.

Colin Hughes, *Lime, Lemon and Sarsaparilla: The Italian Community in South Wales, 1881–1945* (Bridgend, Seren, 1991).

Peter John, 'The Oxford Welsh in the 1930s: a study in class, community and political influence', *Llafur*, 5, 4 (1991), 99–106.

Philip N. Jones, *Colliery Settlement in the South Wales Coalfield, 1850–1926* (Hull, University of Hull, 1969). A very useful survey of housing provision.

Philip N. Jones, 'Workmen's trains in the South Wales coalfield,

1870–1926', *Transport History*, 3 (1970), 21–35. Important for understanding inter-valley mobility.

Dave Lyddon, 'Trade union traditions, the Oxford Welsh and the 1934 Pressed Steel strike', *Llafur*, 6, 2 (1993), 106–14. This essay argues against the importance of the Welsh contribution.

W. D. Rubinstein, 'The anti-Jewish riots of 1911 in south Wales: a re-examination', *Welsh History Review*, 18, 4 (1997), 667–99. An icono-clastic essay challenging the orthodox interpretation of the riots.

Brian Staines, 'The movement of population from south Wales with specific reference to the effects of the Industrial Transference Scheme, 1928–37', in Colin Baber and L. J. Williams (eds.), *Modern South Wales: Essays in Economic History* (Cardiff, University of Wales Press, 1986), 237–49.

Brinley Thomas, 'The migration of labour into the Glamorganshire coalfield, 1861–1911', in Walter E. Minchinton (ed.), *Industrial South Wales 1750–1914: Essays in Welsh Economic History* (London, Frank Cass & Co. Ltd, 1969), 37–56. A classic essay.

Tim Williams, 'The anglicisation of south Wales', in R. Samuel (ed.), *Patriotism*, vol. II (London, Routledge, 1989), 193–203. An icono-clastic account of the erosion of the Welsh language which pulls no punches.

Trade union history

Peter Ackers, 'Colliery deputies in the British coal industry before nationalization', *International Review of Social History*, 39 (1994), 383–414. This essay argues for greater recognition of a usually neglected group of workers.

Robin Page Arnot, *South Wales Miners*, vol. I: *1898–1914* (London, Allen & Unwin, 1967). To be read for the detail, and lengthy citations from original documents.

Robin Page Arnot, *South Wales Miners*, vol. II: *1914–1926* (Cardiff, Cymric Federation Press, 1975).

Martin Barclay, ' "The Slaves of the Lamp": the Aberdare miners' strike, 1910', *Llafur*, 2, 3 (1978), 24–42. An account of a dispute of major significance.

Stuart Broomfield, 'The apprentice boys' strikes of the Second World War', *Llafur*, 3, 2 (1981), 53–67. Change and friction in the wartime coal industry.

Alun Burge, 'In search of Harry Blount: scabbing between the wars in one south Wales community', *Llafur*, 6, 3 (1994), 58–69. A very interesting micro-analysis of the MIU.

E. W. Edwards, 'The Pontypridd area', in Margaret Morris, *The General Strike* (Harmondsworth, Penguin, 1976), 411–25.

Ness Edwards, *The History of the South Wales Miners* (London, Labour Publishing Co., 1926). An account of the years up to 1898.

Ness Edwards, *The History of the South Wales Miners' Federation* (London, Lawrence & Wishart, 1938). This book covers the period 1898–1935.

Eric Wyn Evans, *The Miners of South Wales* (Cardiff, University of Wales Press, 1961). An alternative account of the period up to 1912.

Hywel Francis, 'The anthracite strike and disturbances of 1925', *Llafur*, 1, 2 (1973) (1983 facsimile edn), 53–66.

Hywel Francis, 'South Wales', in Jeffrey Skelley (ed.), *The General Strike, 1926* (1976), 232–60.

Hywel Francis, 'The secret world of the south Wales miner: the relevance of oral history', in David Smith (ed.), *A People and a Proletariat: Essays in the History of Modern Wales, 1780–1980* (London, Pluto Press, 1980), 166–80.

Hywel Francis and Kim Howells, 'The politics of coal in south Wales, 1945–48', *Llafur*, 3, 3 (1982), 74–85.

Hywel Francis and David Smith, *The Fed: A History of the South Wales Miners in the Twentieth Century* (London, Lawrence & Wishart, 1980; reissued Cardiff, University of Wales Press, 1998). A landmark history of the 'union in its society'.

Deian Hopkin, 'The great unrest in Wales, 1910–1913: questions of evidence', in Deian R. Hopkin and Gregory S. Kealey (eds.), *Class, Community and the Labour Movement: Wales and Canada, 1850–1930* (Aberystwyth, Llafur/CCLH, 1989), 249–75. An interesting use of statistics to raise questions about the concept of the 'Great Unrest'.

Paul Jeremy, 'Life on Circular 703: the crisis of destitution in the

South Wales coalfield during the lockout of 1926', *Llafur*, 2, 2 (1977), 65–75. The Ministry of Health's draconian handling of out-relief.

Bill Jones, Brian Roberts and Chris Williams, ' "Going from darkness to the light": south Wales miners' attitudes towards nationalisation', *Llafur*, 7, 1 (1996), 96–110. A response to Zweiniger-Bargielowska's essay (see below).

Ioan Matthews, 'Maes y Glo Carreg ac Undeb y Glöwyr 1872–1925', in Geraint H. Jenkins (ed.), *Cof Cenedl: Ysgrifau ar Hanes Cymru*, 8 (Llandysul, Gomer, 1993), 133–64. This essay looks at the sometimes strained relationship between anthracite miners and the rest of the coalfield.

Ioan Matthews, 'The world of the anthracite miner', *Llafur*, 6, 1 (1992), 96–104. A superb short study of the society of the anthracite coalfield.

Eddie May, 'Labour, capital and the state in the south Wales coalfield, 1912–1921: the case of Gwaun-cae-Gurwen', in Ian Blanchard (ed.), *New Directions in Economic and Social History* (Avonbridge, Newlees Press, 1995), 47–55.

Anthony Mòr O'Brien, 'Patriotism on trial: the strike of the south Wales miners, July 1915', *Welsh History Review*, 12, 1 (1984/5), 76–104. A controversial account of a controversial strike.

Jane Morgan, 'Police and labour in the age of Lindsay, 1910–1936', *Llafur*, 5, 1 (1988), 15–20.

Jane Morgan, *Conflict and Order: The Police and Labour Disputes in England and Wales, 1900–1939* (Oxford, Oxford University Press, 1987).

Will Paynter, 'The "Fed" ', in Goronwy Alun Hughes (ed.), *Men of No Property: Historical Studies of Welsh Trade Unions* (Caerwys, Gwasg Gwenffrwd, 1971), 68–72. Makes important statements regarding SWMF's 'social centrality'.

David Smith, 'The struggle against company unionism in the south Wales coalfield, 1926–1939', *Welsh History Review*, 6, 3 (1973), 354–78.

David Smith, 'Tonypandy 1910: definitions of community', *Past and Present*, 87 (1980), 158–84. A brilliant social history with implications far beyond Mid Rhondda.

Chris Williams, 'The South Wales Miners' Federation', *Llafur*, 5, 3 (1990), 45–56. A historiographical analysis.

Chris Williams, ' "The hope of the British proletariat": the south Wales miners, 1910–1947', in Alan Campbell, Nina Fishman and David Howell (eds.), *Miners, Unions and Politics, 1910–47* (Aldershot, Scolar, 1996), 121–44. A survey article.

Ina-Maria Zweiniger-Bargielowska, 'Miners' militancy: a study of four south Wales collieries during the middle of the twentieth century', *Welsh History Review*, 16, 3 (1992), 356–83. A very interesting analysis of industrial relations, based on four collieries.

Ina-Maria Zweiniger-Bargielowska, 'Colliery managers and nationalisation: the experience in south Wales', *Business History*, 34, 4 (1992), 59–78. An important study of an oft-neglected group.

Ina-Maria Zweiniger-Bargielowska, 'South Wales miners' attitudes towards nationalisation: an essay in oral history', *Llafur*, 6, 3 (1994), 70–84. Essay arguing that miners' rank-and-file showed 'apathy' towards nationalisation.

Politics and ideology

Felix Aubel, 'The Conservatives in Wales, 1880–1935', in Martin Francis and Ina-Maria Zweiniger-Bargielowska (eds.), *The Conservatives and Modern British Society* (Cardiff, University of Wales Press, 1996), 96–110. This has some material on the coalfield.

David Cleaver, 'Labour and Liberals in the Gower constituency, 1885–1910', *Welsh History Review*, 12, 3 (1985), 388–410.

Stephen M. Cullen, 'Another nationalism: the British Union of Fascists in Glamorgan, 1932–40', *Welsh History Review*, 17, 1 (1994), 101–14.

Wayne David, 'The Labour Party and the "exclusion" of the Communists: the case of the Ogmore Divisional Labour Party in the 1920s', *Llafur*, 3, 4 (1983), 5–15. An account of internecine warfare in the Llynfi Valley.

Keith Davies, 'Roughneck in the Rhondda: some ideological connections between the United States and the south Wales coalfield, 1900–1914', *Llafur*, 6, 4 (1995), 80–92. Industrial unionism and the transatlantic connection.

Barry Doyle, 'Who paid the price of patriotism? The funding of Charles Stanton during the Merthyr Boroughs by-election of 1915', *English Historical Review*, 109 (1994), 1215–22.

David Egan, 'The Swansea conference of the British Council of Soldiers' and Workers' Delegates, July 1917: reactions to the Russian Revolution of February 1917, and the anti-war movement in south Wales', *Llafur*, 1, 4 (1975) (1983 facsimile edn), 162–87.

David Egan, 'The Unofficial Reform Committee and *The Miners' Next Step*: documents from the W. H. Mainwaring papers, with an introduction and notes', *Llafur*, 2, 3 (1978), 64–80.

David Egan, ' "A cult of their own": syndicalism and *The Miners' Next Step*', in Alan Campbell, Nina Fishman and David Howell (eds.), *Miners, Unions and Politics, 1910–47* (Aldershot, Scolar, 1996), 13–33.

Nina Fishman, *The British Communist Party and the Trade Unions, 1933–45* (Aldershot, Scolar, 1995). This has some material on south Wales.

Nina Fishman, 'Heroes and anti-heroes: Communists in the coalfields', in Alan Campbell, Nina Fishman and David Howell (eds.), *Miners, Unions and Politics, 1910–47* (Aldershot, Scolar, 1996), 93–117.

Kenneth O. Fox, 'Labour and Merthyr's Khaki Election of 1900', *Welsh History Review*, 2, 4 (1965), 351–66. Keir Hardie's victory.

Hywel Francis, 'Welsh miners and the Spanish Civil War', *Journal of Contemporary History*, 5, 3 (1970), 177–91.

Hywel Francis, *Miners Against Fascism: Wales and the Spanish Civil War* (London, Lawrence & Wishart, 1984). A brilliant, passionate account of 'proletarian internationalism' at its zenith.

David Gilbert, 'Community and municipalism: collective identity in late-Victorian and Edwardian mining towns', *Journal of Historical Geography*, 17, 3 (1991), 257–70. This includes valuable material on the 1917 Commission of Enquiry.

Roy Gregory, *The Miners and British Politics, 1906–1914* (Oxford, Oxford University Press, 1968). Regional emphasis in a study of the politicization of the MFGB.

Pyrs Gruffydd, '"A crusade against consumption": environment, health and social reform in Wales, 1900–1939', *Journal of Historical Geography*, 21, 1 (1995), 39–54. A very stimulating treatment of a key social reform issue.

Bob Holton, *British Syndicalism, 1900–1914* (London, Pluto, 1976). An important, if occasionally over-excitable, study.

Deian Hopkin, 'The rise of Labour: Llanelli, 1890–1922', in Geraint H. Jenkins and J. Beverley Smith (eds.), *Politics and Society in Wales, 1840–1922* (Cardiff, University of Wales Press, 1988), 161–82. A very useful local study.

Deian Hopkin, 'The rise of Labour in Wales, 1890–1914', *Llafur*, 6, 3 (1994), 120–41. This concentrates on the ILP.

Chris Howard, '"Reactionary radicalism: the Mid-Glamorgan bye-election, March 1910', in Stewart Williams (ed.), *Glamorgan Historian*, 9 (1973), 29–41. An account of the significant defeat of Vernon Hartshorn.

Chris Howard, '"Expectations born to death": the local Labour Party expansion in the 1920s', in Jay M. Winter (ed.), *The Working Class in Modern British History: Essays in Honour of Henry Pelling* (Cambridge, Cambridge University Press, 1983), 65–81. The Labour Party's early difficulties; including material on Aberavon.

Chris Howard, '"The focus of the mute hopes of a whole class": Ramsay MacDonald and Aberavon, 1922–29', *Llafur*, 7, 1 (1996), 68–77. An impressive study of local politics.

J. Graham Jones, 'Wales and the "New Socialism", 1926–29', *Welsh History Review*, 11, 2 (1982), 173–99. This advances an interesting argument regarding the interrelationship of the industrial and political wings of the Labour movement.

J. Graham Jones, 'Welsh politics between the wars: the personnel of Labour', *Transactions of the Honourable Society of Cymmrodorion* (1983), 164–83.

Philip N. Jones, 'The South Wales Regional Survey, 1921: a reassessment after sixty years', *Cambria*, 8, 2 (1981), 17–31.

Richard Lewis, *Leaders and Teachers: Adult Education and the Challenge of Labour in South Wales, 1906–1940* (Cardiff, University of Wales Press, 1993). An outstanding history of a distinctive feature of the coalfield.

Richard Lewis, 'The Welsh radical tradition and the ideal of a democratic popular culture', in Eugenio F. Biagini (ed.), *Citizenship and Community: Liberals, Radicals and Collective Identities in the British Isles, 1865–1931* (Cambridge, Cambridge University Press, 1996), 325–40. An important overview of the Welsh intellectual response to social problems.

Stuart Macintyre, *Little Moscows: Communism and Working-Class Militancy in Inter-war Britain* (London, Croom Helm, 1980). This includes a chapter on Mardy.

Stuart Macintyre, *A Proletarian Science: Marxism in Britain, 1917–1933* (Cambridge, Cambridge University Press, 1986). The political thought and culture of the Communist Party of Great Britain.

Eddie May, 'Coal, community, town planning and the management of labour', *Planning Perspectives*, 11 (1996), 145–66. An original investigation of Welsh intellectuals' approaches to urban space.

Eddie May, 'Charles Stanton and the limits to "patriotic' labour"', *Welsh History Review*, 18, 3 (1996), 145–66. This puts Stanton's 1915 victory in Merthyr in a longer-term context.

Kenneth O. Morgan, 'Democratic politics in Glamorgan, 1884–1914', *Morgannwg*, 4 (1960), 5–27. This stresses the importance of local studies to an understanding of political history.

Kenneth O. Morgan, *Wales in British Politics, 1868–1922* (Cardiff, University of Wales Press, 1980 edn). More a history of Liberal than of Labour Wales, its judgements have stood the test of time.

Kenneth O. Morgan, *Modern Wales: Politics, Places and People* (Cardiff, University of Wales Press, 1995). A collection of essays from the master of Welsh political history.

Anthony Mòr O'Brien, 'The Merthyr Boroughs election, November 1915', *Welsh History Review*, 12, 4 (1985), 538–66. This provides an interpretation, since challenged, of this episode.

Dylan Morris, 'Sosialaeth i'r Cymry – trafodaeth yr ILP', *Llafur*, 4, 2 (1985), 51–63. This assesses how Welsh and (largely Welsh-speaking) socialists handled the question of Welsh nationality.

Jon Parry, 'Labour leaders and local politics, 1888–1902: the example of Aberdare', *Welsh History Review*, 14, 3 (1989), 399–416. A local study.

Peter Stead, 'Working class leadership in south Wales, 1900–1920', *Welsh History Review*, 6, 3 (1973), 329–53. An essay looking at traditions of trade union and political leadership, and stressing continuity rather than upheaval.

Peter Stead, *Coleg Harlech: The First Fifty Years* (Cardiff, University of Wales Press, 1977). An important history of both the vision behind, and reality of, Wales's adult education college.

Peter Stead, 'The language of Edwardian politics', in David Smith (ed.), *A People and a Proletariat: Essays in the History of Wales, 1780–1980* (London, Pluto Press, 1980), 148–65. This essay examines the divergent approaches of socialists and Lib-Labs to the issues of the time.

Peter Stead, 'Establishing a heartland: the Labour Party in Wales', in Kenneth D. Brown (ed.), *The First Labour Party* (Beckenham, Croom Helm, 1985), 64–88. The early history of the Labour Party.

Duncan Tanner, *Political Change and the Labour Party, 1900–18* (Cambridge, Cambridge University Press, 1990). An authoritative examination of politics with a heavy regional emphasis.

Duncan Tanner, 'The Labour Party and electoral politics in the coalfields', in Alan Campbell, Nina Fishman and David Howell (eds.), *Miners, Unions and Politics, 1910–47* (Aldershot, Scolar, 1996), 59–92. The 'miners' vote' in context.

Chris Williams, ' "An able administrator of capitalism"? The Labour Party in the Rhondda, 1917–21', *Llafur*, 4, 4 (1987), 20–33. This explores tensions within the Labour Party.

Chris Williams, *Democratic Rhondda: Politics and Society, 1885–1951* (Cardiff, University of Wales Press, 1996). A detailed study of politics, parliamentary and local.

Chris Williams, 'Democracy and nationalism in Wales: the Lib-Lab enigma', in Robert Stradling, Scott Newton and David Bates (eds.), *Conflict and Coexistence: Nationalism and Democracy in Modern Europe: Essays in Honour of Harry Hearder* (Cardiff, University of Wales Press, 1997), 107–31. A reassessment of the Lib-Labs, and of their relationship with the Cymru Fydd movement.

Siân Rhiannon Williams, 'The Bedwellty Board of Guardians and the Default Act of 1927', *Llafur*, 2, 4 (1979), 65–77. This tells the story of the rebel Guardians.

Autobiography, Biography, Literature

Bert Coombes, *These Poor Hands: The Autobiography of a Miner Working in South Wales* (London, Victor Gollancz, 1939). An evocative, almost 'documentary', autobiography that oozes authenticity.

James A. Davies (ed.), *The Heart of Wales: An Anthology* (Bridgend, Seren, 1994). A selection of literary excerpts.

Paul Davies, *A. J. Cook*, (Manchester, Manchester University Press, 1987). An important study.

Wil Jon Edwards, *From the Valley I Came* (London, Angus and Robertson, 1956). An insightful autobiography.

David Egan, 'Abel Morgan 1878–1972', *Llafur*, 1, 2 (1973) (1983 facsimile edn), 67–71. A tribute to an ordinary, but exceptional, local figure.

David Egan, 'Noah Ablett, 1883–1935', *Llafur*, 4, 3 (1986), 19–30. This essay surveys Ablett's political and intellectual attitudes.

E. L. Ellis, *T. J.: A Life of Dr Thomas Jones, CH* (Cardiff, University of Wales Press, 1992). A very impressive biography.

Eric Wyn Evans, *Mabon (William Abraham 1842–1922): A Study in Trade Union Leadership* (Cardiff, University of Wales Press, 1959). An orthodox account of the early giant.

Michael Foot, *Aneurin Bevan*, vol. I: *1897–1945* (London, Mac-Gibbon & Kee, 1962). One of the great biographies, whatever its flaws.

James Griffiths, *Pages from Memory* (London, J. M. Dent & Sons, 1969). An over-romantic autobiography.

Robert Griffiths, *S. O. Davies: A Socialist Faith* (Llandysul, Gomer, 1983). Homage to one of the SWMF's central figures of the 1930s.

Frank Hodges, *My Adventures as a Labour Leader* (London, George Newnes, 1925). A knockabout narrative from the mercurial miners' leader turning coalowner.

Arthur Horner, *Incorrigible Rebel* (London, MacGibbon & Kee, 1960). A restrained account of a fascinating life.

Lewis Jones, *Cwmardy* (London, Lawrence & Wishart, 1978 edn). A raw but gripping first novel by the Rhondda communist.

Lewis Jones, *We Live* (London, Lawrence & Wishart, 1978 edn). His posthumously published second novel.

Will Paynter, *My Generation* (London, Allen & Unwin, 1972). An impressive autobiography by one of the key figures in the history of the south Wales miners.

Robert Pitt, 'Educator and agitator: Charlie Gibbons, 1888–1967', *Llafur*, 5, 2 (1989), 72–83. The life and times of a famous syndicalist-cum-Communist.

David Smith, *Lewis Jones* (Cardiff, University of Wales Press, 1982). A short, fascinating study of the novelist.

J. Beverley Smith (ed.), *James Griffiths and His Times* (Ferndale, W. T. Maddock, 1977). This includes reminiscences by Griffiths, and an excellent essay by the editor.

Peter Stead, 'Vernon Hartshorn: miners' agent and cabinet minister', in Stewart Williams (ed.), *Glamorgan Historian*, 6 (1970), 83–94. A biographical study of one of south Wales's premier figures.

Meic Stephens (ed.), *A Rhondda Anthology* (Bridgend, Seren, 1993). A selection of literary excerpts.

County and community studies

T. Brennan, E. W. Cooney and H. Pollins, *Social Change in South-West Wales* (London, Watts & Co., 1954). A social survey of the Swansea area that retains value.

Russell Davies, *Secret Sins: Sex, Violence and Society in Carmarthenshire, 1870–1920* (Cardiff, University of Wales Press, 1996). A superb social history of a county on the fringe of the coalfield; the work is inspired by the *Annales* movement.

Joe England, 'The Merthyr of the twentieth century: a postscript', in Glanmor Williams (ed.), *Merthyr Politics: the Making of a Radical Tradition* (Cardiff, University of Wales Press, 1966), 82–101.

K. S. Hopkins (ed.), *Rhondda Past and Future* (Ferndale, Rhondda Borough Council, 1975). This volume contains significant contributions by David Smith and Hywel Francis.

Arthur H. John and Glanmor Williams (eds.), *Glamorgan County*

History, vol. V: *Industrial Glamorgan* (Cardiff, Glamorgan County History Trust Ltd, 1980). An immensely important county history with key essays on the economy.

E. D. Lewis, *The Rhondda Valleys* (Cardiff, University College Cardiff Press, 1984 edn). A classic socio-economic study of the archetypal mining valley.

Michael Lieven, *Senghennydd: The Universal Pit Village, 1890–1930* (Llandysul, Gomer, 1994). A fascinating, popular social history of a community made notorious by two tragic explosions; it is stimulating on gender relations.

Alun Morgan, 'Bedlinog: glimpses of a pre-war society', *Glamorgan Historian*, 11 (1975), 137–48. Insights into the turbulent history of one settlement.

Prys Morgan (ed.), *Glamorgan County History*, vol. VI: *Glamorgan Society 1780–1980* (Cardiff, Glamorgan County History Trust Ltd, 1988). This volume includes valuable contributions by Ieuan Gwynedd Jones, J. Graham Jones, Philip N. Jones and Hywel Francis in particular.

Brian Roberts, 'A mining town in wartime: the fears for the future', *Llafur*, 6, 1 (1992), 82–95. A summary of the Mass Observation report of 1942 on Blaina.

Popular culture and religion

Christopher Baggs, 'Well done Cymmer workmen! The Cymmer Collieries Workmen's Library', *Llafur*, 5, 3 (1990), 20–7.

Hywel Francis, 'The origins of the South Wales Miners' Library', *History Workshop Journal*, 2 (1976), 183–205. This essay has much to offer on the intellectual culture of the coalfield.

Angela Gaffney, 'Monuments and memory: the Great War in Wales', in Julie Arnold, Kate Davies and Simon Ditchfield (eds.), *History and Heritage: Consuming the Past in Contemporary Culture* (Shaftesbury, Donhead, 1998), 79–89. An original overview of the process of remembrance.

C. E. Gwyther, 'Sidelights on religion and politics in the Rhondda Valley, 1906–1926', *Llafur*, 3, 1 (1980), 30–43.

Bert Hogenkamp, 'Miners' cinemas in south Wales in the 1920s and 1930s', *Llafur*, 4, 2 (1985), 64–76.

David J. V. Jones, *Crime and Policing in the Twentieth Century: The South Wales Experience* (Cardiff, University of Wales Press, 1996). This book includes much of interest to the historian of the coalfield.

E. D. Lewis and I. G. Jones, 'Capel y Cymer: Llanw a Thrai', *Morgannwg*, 25 (1981), 137–63. A social history of an individual chapel.

Robert Pope, *Building Jerusalem: Nonconformity, Labour and the Social Question in Wales, 1906–1939* (Cardiff, University of Wales Press, 1998). This work concentrates on the intellectual response of Welsh Nonconformity.

D. Ben Rees, *Chapels in the Valley: A Study in the Sociology of Welsh Nonconformity* (Upton, Ffynnon Press, 1975). This may be quarried for historical material.

Stephen Ridgwell, 'South Wales and the cinema in the 1930s', *Welsh History Review*, 17, 4 (1995), 590–615. A useful survey.

Dai [David] Smith, *Wales! Wales?* (London, Allen & Unwin, 1984). An interrogation of the culture and politics of modern Welsh identity.

Dai [David] Smith, *Aneurin Bevan and the World of South Wales* (Cardiff, University of Wales Press, 1993). A central chapter on Bevan is surrounded by collected essays dealing with culture, politics and society: essential reading.

David Smith and Gareth Williams, *Fields of Praise: The Official History of the Welsh Rugby Union, 1881–1981* (Cardiff, University of Wales Press, 1980). Magnificent social history of Wales's premier sporting passion.

Peter Stead, 'The voluntary response to mass unemployment in south Wales', in Walter E. Minchinton (ed.), *Reactions to Social and Economic Change, 1750–1939* (Exeter, University of Exeter, 1979), 97–117.

Christopher Turner, 'Conflicts of faith? Religion and labour in Wales, 1890–1914', in Deian R. Hopkin and Gregory S. Kealey (eds.), *Class, Community and the Labour Movement: Wales and Canada* (Aberystwyth, Llafur/CCLH, 1989), 67–85.

Gareth Williams, *1905 and All That: Essays on Rugby Football, Sport and Welsh Society* (Llandysul, Gomer, 1991). A highly perceptive collection of essays.

Gender relations

Deirdre Beddoe, 'Images of Welsh women', in Tony Curtis (ed.), *Wales: The Imagined Nation: Studies in Cultural and National Identity* (Bridgend, Poetry Wales Press, 1986), 225–38. This essay dissects the myth of the 'Welsh Mam'.

Sue Bruley, 'A woman's right to work? The role of women in the unemployed movement between the wars', in Sybil Oldfield (ed.), *This Working-Day World: Women's Lives and Culture(s) in Britain, 1914–1945* (London, Taylor & Francis, 1994), 40–53. This includes material on south Wales.

Rosemary Crook, 'Tidy women: women in the Rhondda between the wars', *Oral History Journal*, 10 (1982), 40–6. A preliminary survey of women's attitudes, concentrating on notions of respectability.

Neil Evans and Dot Jones, ' "A blessing for the miner's wife": the campaign for pithead baths in the south Wales coalfield, 1908–1950', *Llafur*, 6, 3 (1994), 5–28. This essay interweaves official and popular perspectives to good effect.

Hywel Francis, ' "Say nothing and leave in the middle of the night", *History Workshop Journal*, 32 (1991), 69–76. This essay revisits volunteering for Spain, from a gender perspective.

Diana Gittins, *Fair Sex: Family Size and Structure, 1900–39* (London, Hutchinson, 1982). This includes material on south Wales.

Graham Goode and Sara Delamont, 'Opportunity denied: the voices of the lost grammar school girls of the inter-war years', in Sandra Betts (ed.), *Our Daughters' Land: Past and Present* (Cardiff, University of Wales Press, 1996), 103–24.

Angela V. John, 'A miner struggle? Women's protests in Welsh mining history', *Llafur*, 4, 1 (1984), 72–90. This makes the case for a study of gender relations in the coalfield.

Angela V. John (ed.), *Our Mothers' Land: Chapters in Welsh Women's History, 1830–1939* (Cardiff, University of Wales Press, 1991). A ground-breaking collection, including essays by Dot Jones on women in the Rhondda Valleys, and by Kay Cook and Neil Evans on the women's suffrage movement in Wales.

Dot Jones, 'Serfdom and slavery: women's work in Wales, 1890–1930', in Deian R. Hopkin and Gregory S. Kealey (eds.), *Class, Community and the Labour Movement: Wales and Canada* (Aberystwyth, Llafur/CCLH, 1989), 86–100. An important essay contrasting Rhondda and Cardiganshire.

Sheila Owen-Jones, 'Women in the tinplate industry: Llanelli, 1930–1950', *Oral History Journal*, 15, 1 (1987), 42–9. A preliminary survey based on oral testimony.

Jane Pilcher, 'Who should do the dishes? Three generations of Welsh women talking about men and housework', in Jane Aaron, Teresa Rees, Sandra Betts and Moira Vincentelli (eds.), *Our Sisters' Land: The Changing Identities of Women in Wales* (Cardiff, University of Wales Press, 1994), 31–47.

Gillian Scott, 'A "trade union for married women": the Women's Co-operative Guild, 1914–1920', in Sybil Oldfield (ed.), *This Working-Day World: Women's Lives and Culture(s) in Britain, 1914–1945* (London, Taylor & Francis, 1994), 18–28. A preliminary, British-level survey of this important organization.

Leigh Verrill-Rhys and Deirdre Beddoe (eds.), *Parachutes and Petticoats: Welsh Women Writing on the Second World War* (Dinas Powys, Honno, 1992). An anthology of women's writing.

Catherine Welsby, ' "Warning her as to her future behaviour": the lives of the widows of the Senghenydd mining disaster of 1913', *Llafur*, 6, 4 (1995), 93–109. Gender relations and moral attitudes in microcosm, in the management and distribution of relief funds.

Carol White and Siân Rhiannon Williams (eds.), *Struggle or Starve: Women's Lives in the South Wales Valleys Between the Two World Wars* (Dinas Powys, Honno, 1998). An anthology of women's writing with an excellent introduction.

Mari A. Williams, ' *"Where is Mrs Jones going?" Women and the Second World War in South Wales'* (Aberystwyth, University of Wales Centre for Advanced Welsh and Celtic Studies, 1995). This concentrates on women's work in munitions factories.

Mari A. Williams, 'Yr ymgyrch i "Achub y Mamau" yng nghymoedd diwydiannol de Cymru, 1918–1939', in Geraint H. Jenkins (ed.), *Cof Cenedl: Ysgrifau ar Hanes Cymru*, vol. XI (Llandysul, Gomer, 1996), 117–46. An account of campaigns for maternity and child welfare services.

Index